Faith in Science
Scientists search for truth

Edited by
W. Mark Richardson
and Gordy Slack

with a foreword by Ian Barbour

London and New York

First published 2001 by Routledge
11 New Fetter Lane, London EC4P 4EE
Simultaneously published in the USA and Canada
by Routledge
29 West 35th Street, New York, NY 10001

Routledge is an imprint of the Taylor & Francis Group

© 2001 W. Mark Richardson and Gordy Slack

Typeset in Sabon by Taylor & Francis Books Ltd
Printed and bound in Great Britain by TJ International Ltd,
Padstow, Cornwall

British Library Cataloguing in Publication Data
A catalogue record for this book is available from the British
Library

Library of Congress Cataloging in Publication Data
Faith in science: scientists search for truth/edited by W. Mark
Richardson and Gordy Slack.
Includes bibliographical references and index.
Contents: A priest at work/John Rodwell–The language of
matter/Brian Cantwell Smith–Parallel evolution/Francisco
Ayala–Molecular grace/Pauline Rudd–Reading God's
signs/Bruno Guiderdoni–The elegant universe/Arno
Penzias–Virtually sacred/Mark Pesce–The ladder to
God/Mehdi Golshani–Just, loving, and random God/Kenneth
Kendler–Do androids dream of bread and wine?/Anne
Foerst–Transcendental theory/Joel Primack–Testing faith,
wrestling with mystery/Charles Townes.
1. Religion and science. 2. Scientists–interviews. 3.
Scientists–Religious life. I. Richardson, W. Mark, 1949– II.
Slack, Gordy.
BL241 .F35 2001
291.1'75–dc21   2001019957

ISBN 0–415–25764–6 (hbk)
ISBN 0–415–25765–4 (pbk)

Contents

Foreword

Ian Barbour

The common stereotype portrays religion and science as inescapably in conflict. On the one side are biblical literalists who believe in God but not evolution. On the other are atheistic scientists who believe in evolution but not God. In reality, however, there is a great diversity of views in both the scientific and the religious community today.

There are of course many scientists who are atheists or who are totally uninterested in religion. A career in science can be very demanding and scientists are often preoccupied with their research. They seldom talk to each other about their religious or philosophical beliefs. But a significant number of scientists are members of traditional religious communities, and their views range from conservative to liberal. Others are not participants in religious institutions but do express a deep personal spirituality. A response of awe and wonder at the beauty, grandeur and complexity of the universe is not uncommon among the scientists who examine it so closely. Some scientists see religious implications in the intelligibility of the world or in particular scientific discoveries such as the Big Bang in cosmology. Others seek views of human consciousness and the unity of the person that might provide an alternative to both the classical dualism of soul and body (or mind and body) and the account offered by reductive materialism.

Some scientists assert that the scientific method is the only reliable form of understanding; they claim that only what can be studied by science is real and causally effective. Others hold that both science and religion are significant enterprises but that they differ radically from each other; science asks about lawful regularities among natural phenomena whereas religion asks about meaning and purpose in a wider interpretive framework. They suggest that science can tell us what is possible in technological applications, but not what is desirable. Advances in genetic engineering and computer science, for instance, give us new powers over the future that raise profound ethical, philosophical and theological questions that the sciences themselves are not equipped to answer. Cosmology, too, leads to questions at the boundaries of science. Why is there a universe at all? Why does it have the particular laws it has? And why are these laws intelligible to us?

Indicative of the growing interest in the relationship between science and religion was the establishment in 1995 of the Program of Dialogue in Science, Ethics and Religion within the most prominent organization of US scientists, the American Association for the Advancement of Science (AAAS). The program has been active in planning workshops, conferences, publications and multiple sessions at annual meetings of the AAAS. The British Association for the Advancement of Science has also held sessions on science and religion at their annual meetings. Scientists in a growing number of colleges and universities have joined with historians, philosophers and scholars of religion in offering lectures and courses on science and religion. The average number of books published annually in the United States and listed under the Library of Congress heading "Religion and Science" tripled from the 1950s to the 1990s.

Among the centers around the world devoted to the exciting new dialogue between scientists and scholars of religion none has had a more outstanding record of publication, graduate-level teaching, workshops and conferences than the Center for Theology and the Natural Sciences (CTNS) in the Graduate Theological Union, an ecumenical consortium adjacent to the Berkeley campus of the University of California. In 1996, CTNS initiated a program called Science and the Spiritual Quest (SSQ) with the help of a grant from the John Templeton Foundation. This program was unique in bringing outstanding scientists together to examine the relation of science and religion in their own lives, thereby encouraging personal reflection as well as intellectual inquiry. SSQ defined religion broadly to include forms of spirituality that are not dependent on traditional religious institutions. The phrase "spiritual quest" allowed the inclusion of persons interested in tentative and open-ended exploration as well as those with a life-long commitment to a particular religious tradition. The interviews included in this volume were conducted as part of the SSQ project and the participants used them as the basis for discussion in groups divided according to their specialty: physics, cosmology, the biological sciences and computer science. Many of them later presented their conclusions at a public conference in Berkeley.

The interviews published in this volume offer penetrating reflections by distinguished research scientists. With the interviewers, they explore the spiritual dimensions of their lives and their work, describing their intellectual, religious and personal journeys and their internal dialogues concerning the relation between their scientific and spiritual interests. They recount crucial events in their personal and professional lives, describing moments of breakthrough and realization as well as moments of doubt. They explore the ethical concerns related to their scientific work, and discuss the influence their spiritual commitments have on their ethical judgments.

For some of these men and women, science is a way of understanding God's creation and therefore a form of worship. Several of the physicists see religious implications in the "fine-tuning" of the parameters of the early universe; if the expansion rate had been even a tiny bit faster or slower, the universe would have dispersed or re-collapsed before planets and life and consciousness could have arisen. But several of these authors are highly critical of classical concepts of God. Some combine the practices of more than one tradition (Judaism and Zen Buddhism, for instance). Still others want to stay close to religious experience and hold that we cannot meaningfully say very much about God. Some think that in the future the sacred may be found in new places such as humanoid robots or virtual environments in interactive computers. Classical problems are here confronted in new contexts, such as the problem of freedom and determinism raised now by behavioral genetics – are we determined by our genes? – or the ancient problem of reconciling undeserved suffering and a just and powerful God.

The skill of the interviewers is also impressive. The most exciting territories are not always the most comfortable to explore, but Gordy Slack and Philip Clayton press for further clarification, request examples of generalizations, and draw the collection together by asking for reactions to statements by other scientists. The conversations move at a pace that covers a wide range of important issues in a brief span of time. While these interviews are fascinating in their own right, they also contribute to a significant new approach to both ecumenical exchange and the science–religion dialogue.

Introduction

W. Mark Richardson

We marvel at the success and power of contemporary science and the countless ways it is transforming our lives. But rarely do we note that the science of today can be traced back to the cultures of Western monotheism – Christianity, Judaism and Islam. On the surface this connection seems odd, even distant, especially under the apparent strain between religion and science in our day. But beneath the veneer of estrangement remain deep family ties between the scientific pursuit of truths about the material world and the spiritual quest to comprehend its significance and to find the rightful place for humans in it. These family ties, some ancient, others brand new, some practical, others philosophical, are at the heart of this book.

The men and women interviewed here represent a diverse cross-section of the highest strata of scientific accomplishment. Some are physicists, others biologists, cosmologists, or computer scientists. Some are Muslims, others Jews, and others Christians. Still others fall squarely into none of these traditional religious categories. The one thing they do all have in common is a willingness to explore openly the interface between their science and the fundamental orientations and perspectives embodied in their spiritual or religious quests. They all explore how spiritual experiences have influenced their professional work, and conversely, how perspective gained through the sciences has influenced their understanding of the great religious themes about God, about the nature of persons as moral and spiritual agents, and about purpose and meaning in the universe.

The scientists in this book find no single answer to the questions posed at the juncture of science and religion. Rather, the interviews reveal the many subtle and complex factors that shape the relationship between scientific and religious pursuits of truth. The variety of understandings among people who share as much in common as scientists do is a large part of the story told by this book. Each appreciates the mutual influence of science and religion in his or her own way, some acknowledging a high degree of integration, others seeing complementary relations but real differences in the modes of knowing and objects of knowledge, and still others remaining skeptical that the two domains of their lives brush against each other at all. Indeed, the approaches taken and conclusions reached by the scientists are as diverse as their backgrounds. Even scientists who share as much as Charles Townes and Arno Penzias do (both are physicists with Nobel Prizes) take radically different approaches to combining their science and religion in a single life. While Penzias says the complete lack of God's thumbprint in the world is the strongest argument for His existence (and His good taste), Townes stresses the power of his own direct experience with the divine. The differences grow from there. Mark Pesce, a leading software innovator and a pagan, sees no division between the science he does and the spiritual meaning he seeks; he is dedicated to making cyberspace, the realm of his science, a sacred place. Theologian and computer scientist Anne Foerst helped to build robots at MIT's Artificial Intelligence Lab. She speculates about baptizing her electronic creations and about when turning them off will violate the commandment against murder. Brian Cantwell Smith is a "hacker-philosopher" who thinks computer science may put meaning back in matter, fusing science and religion together once again.

As diverse as these scientists are, recurring threads do run through the interviews. Indeed, they make another thing crystal clear: the classic questions of past ages remain central in our own, despite scientific progress. Psychiatrist Kenneth Kendler and others, for instance, wrestle with the brutal reality of apparently indiscriminate pain and suffering against the backdrop of faith in God's goodness. Others struggle to understand the apparent contradiction of nature's unremitting regularity and our own undeniable experience of freedom. What role does God play in a world governed by physical law? And how skeptically should we view our basic trust in the *purpose and meaning* of life and the universe, over and against the ambiguity of natural evidence for it, and given science's methodological resistance even to look for it?

Almost all wrestle with the truth status of spiritual insight, and with the wisdom of tradition: these notions resonate deeply in human experience, yet they lack the rigorous testability or precision we demand in the sciences.

Many of the scientists interviewed here acknowledge the limited range and status of the knowledge achieved through their work, as well as the evolving nature of scientific knowledge altogether. As a consequence, spiritual wisdom seems to make use of, but also stand somewhat free from, this changing process. Steady-state cosmology, evolution and deterministic Newtonian physics have all been perceived as threats to religious doctrine. But scientific theories come and go, and although some may ultimately prove correct and others false, their fallibility and shifting nature may soften our distress at inconsistencies between the scientific world view of the day and long-held perspectives rooted in religious tradition. Charles Townes, for example, when asked why God doesn't show up in physicists' equations, dryly points out that the equations are not complete: "There is a great deal we don't yet understand. And there are inconsistencies within science itself, yet we continue to believe it."

Some researchers remark on the limits of science. What science does, it does well. But that, they say, is precisely because of the strictly prescribed kinds of progress we expect from it. As evolutionary biologist Francisco Ayala says, science may one day provide a complete and accurate description of the entire physical world, including the human body, but it will always leave many of life's most pressing questions completely untouched.

Iranian physicist Mehdi Golshani agrees. Science can take the seeker far, he says, but to reach ultimate understanding he or she must engage in metaphysical and religious insight. Without these latter modes of knowing, says Golshani, even the scientific genius is left stranded atop the high ladder of information with nowhere meaningful to go.

The theme of religion's *moral* center surfaces often in the interviews, with several of the scientists finding the heart of spirituality to be in its practical bearing. Many of the scientists strive, too, to use their religious and spiritual insight as an ethical guide to their scientific careers, not so much for scientific inspiration, but to help them make moral decisions as scientists. Mark Pesce, for instance, sees great potential for both good and harm in the virtual reality computer technology he develops. It is his responsibility, as dictated by his spiritual compass and as empowered by his religious practice, to try to influence it for the good.

Religion, others say, has its limits as well. It may eloquently address the meaning of life and the rightful role of humans in it. It may offer millennia of accumulated wisdom about the ways toward fulfillment and meaning and harmony. But on atomic structure, speciation, the roots of diabetes, or the formation of galaxies and black holes, it is either mute or misleading. Some, such as Brian Cantwell Smith and botanist and Anglican priest John Rodwell, wish for the major spiritual traditions to recover an open and inquisitive spirit, and through this to restore their vitality. They fear that religions, locked in dogmas that are insulated from lived experience, will lose their power to interpret modern life at all.

In light of how hot the conflict between evolution and creationism burns in popular culture, especially in the United States, there is a surprising lack of heat on the subject among these scientists. No one interviewed seemed burdened on a philosophical or spiritual level by the implications of Darwinian biology for the special status of persons and their relationship to God. Perhaps the group was self-selecting in this regard. The truth is, there are not many creationists at the top levels of science today, certainly not in biology or genetics. Creationists say this is because scientists who question evolution are locked out of the debate, left marginalized and unpromoted in mainstream academe. Darwinists might even agree: denial of evolution's main tenets disqualifies scientists from serious biological discourse in the same way that flat-Earthers are not invited to high-level debates about astronomy or geology.

Is the Bible's account of creation, including human origins, wrong, then? No, says Darwinist Francisco Ayala, no more than Shakespeare is wrong when he says that his love is a rose. The Bible, these religious scientists seem to agree, is not a scientific textbook, and to treat it like one does credit neither to science nor to religion.

A word about how these interviews came to be:

In 1997, sixty leading scientists from around the world met in workshops in Berkeley, California, to discuss the relationship between their professional work and major themes from some of the world's great spiritual traditions. The scientists were encouraged to bring the spirit of open, hypothetical inquiry, typical of the process of their scientific work, into discussions involving moral and spiritual topics.

The results of these workshop discussions and individual research were presented at a public conference in June, 1998, on the campus of the University of California at Berkeley. There, twenty-seven of the participating scientists presented the findings of their research. Never before had such a distinguished group of scientists convened to speak about science and spirituality.

While it is certainly not rare for scientists to be influenced by religion, it is very unusual, perhaps unprecedented, for them to meet with dozens of colleagues from different fields and traditions to reflect on the relationship between these aspects of their lives. Something special occurs when scholars and scientists are encouraged to give utterance to ideas, and to think through the implications of their work *together* rather than pursue such work in private. Through trust, and through an open exploratory process, these discussions drew out of each person insights that private reflection could not.

Time was also set aside for workshop participants to be interviewed at length by Sonama State University philosophy professor Philip Clayton and science writer Gordy Slack. The interviews in this book, which are original and creative contributions presented here for the first time, are the result of those conversations. Highlights from the conference are gathered in a companion to this volume, entitled *Science and the Spiritual Quest: New Essays by Leading Scientists*.

1 Francisco Ayala

Parallel Evolution

Francisco Ayala is the Donald Bren Professor of biology and a professor of philosophy at the University of California at Irvine. He is the author of 15 books and more than 700 articles on genetics and evolution. In 1960, while still living in his native Spain, Ayala was ordained a Dominican priest. But by later that year he had met the famed Columbia University geneticist Theodosius Dobzhansky, and by 1961 he was in New York City and on the fast track to a doctorate in genetic biology. In 1980, he was inducted into the National Academy of Sciences for his work on population genetics. In 1981, he joined Harvard evolutionary biologist Stephen J. Gould on the front pages of America's news-papers when he testified for the defense in *McLean* vs *Arkansas Board of Education*. In 1994 Ayala served as president of the American Association for the Advancement of Science and from 1994 to 2001 he served on President Clinton's Scientific Advisory Committee. Last year, a profile in the *New York Times* described Ayala as "the Renaissance man of evolutionary biology."

As a former priest who is also dedicated to the teaching of evolution, Ayala is often asked about conflicts between evolu-tionary explanations and those in Genesis. Just as Copernicus' revelations did not undermine the sixteenth-century religious perspective – though many feared it would – Darwin's need not undermine ours, says Ayala. Science and religion present two sepa-rate ways of knowing, not unlike science and art or science and literature. On the other hand, insisting that the Book of Genesis is unscientific would be like telling Shakespeare that his love is not a rose.

Science may well some day explain the entire natural world, Ayala says, but it will always leave many of the most pressing human questions untouched. It is the approaches religion provides to those questions – about life's meaning, about our relationships to one another and to the rest of the universe, about responsibility – that makes it so irreplaceable an ingredient in human life.

FRANCISCO AYALA: My interest in religion, and particularly the interface between religion and science, stems from my belief that religion plays an important role in the lives of most people, so that any satisfactory and fulfilling view of the world has to integrate a religious view. My own concerns and activity are primarily centered around a scientific view of the world. But I don't believe for a moment that science tells us all that is worth saying about the world. It just happens to be the activity to which I have dedicated my professional life, and I find it rewarding and enlightening and fulfilling. But to the extent that society at large wants science to be part of a world view, this has to be done within a context that includes religion.

In the United States many people object to science education in the schools, because they think it conveys a materialistic view of the world. Many additional problems arise from the fact that so many people, and not only common people, perceive a conflict between science and religion. One could go back decades ago to people like Bertrand Russell, the great philosopher, who wrote about the warfare between science and religion. There are scientists in our midst, whom I know, who are dear friends and people I respect, who go as far as to claim that one reason they pursue science is because they hope to obliterate religion. The other side of the coin is even more common. There are people who think that it is unfortunate that science has so much credibility, because they believe that religion needs to get rid of the materialistic view they see as propounded by science.

But science has a lot to offer to society. Certainly it is a very successful way of knowing. Yet I must say once more with no equivocation that I don't think it's the only way of knowing.

GORDY SLACK: Or the only valuable way of knowing?

AYALA: Right. But it is a very important way of knowing and one of great consequence in practical life. Most of modern technology is directly related to science. Much of industrial and economic development is directly related to science. Science is a very powerful way of knowing with consequences that impact our daily lives. And yet, when polls are taken of the public at large, we find that most American citizens are illiterate with respect to science. Half of the US citizens don't know that the Earth goes around the Sun once a year. A majority believe that mankind was created a few thousand years ago just as it now exists. They do not accept that we may have evolved from non-human beings. Well, this is scientific illiteracy.

And illiteracy of any kind is evil. And education is good. I have to confess my prejudice there. I believe knowledge and education are positive values. I think that one reason for the need – not the only reason, but a very important one – for scientific literacy, is to correct the perception of so many people, sometimes even teachers, and certainly many children in the schools, that there is a fundamental conflict between science and religion. Curiously, most people respect what scientists do because they see the great practical and economic benefits that ensue, but they conclude that somehow much of science must be wrong because they believe that many conclusions of science contradict their religious beliefs.

At the University at California at Irvine we get some of the best students in California. We only accept the top 12 percent of the high school graduates, so one would expect them to have better science education than the average. Yet, at the introductory biology class that I teach each year to over 1,000 students, a majority arrive persuaded that if they were to accept what I am teaching, evolution in particular, they would have to reject their religious beliefs. That leads to a very unfortunate dilemma, because they are learning about the origin of species and of humans, and writing the correct answers in the exams, but with great discomfort and even doubts, at least at first. Gradually, through their years in college, they come to accept science. But because of the perceived conflict with which they started, some conclude they must now reject their religious beliefs.

The students' perceived conflict between science and religion stands at this moment very vivid in my mind, because just two days ago I had lunch with an undergraduate in her third or fourth year at UCI who very much wanted to talk with me about these matters. She had been very religious – I knew because of conversations we held when she was a freshman in my introductory biology class – but she now thought that her religious beliefs were untenable. What was the solution to her conflict? I tried to persuade her, as so many others, of my conviction that science and religion deal with two different realms of human experience. Scientific knowledge is one way of knowing; religious experience and religious knowledge are another. There is not necessarily a conflict between them. Indeed, one may see them as two complementary dimensions of human life.

In many ways the perceived conflict between religion and science is the same as if somebody said that studying the humanities or becoming sophisticated in art appreciation would contradict the conclusions of science. Obviously, literature and art are valid ways of knowing about the world and about human life, even if different from science. I try to convey to students that they can both be religious and have a good science education.

SLACK: It's not surprising to me that your students feel this conflict between the study of evolution and their religious upbringing. So much popular discussion and so much debate among scientists and philosophers poses this opposition. It is common to hear in discussions about evolutionary biology that religious thinking obscures Darwin's main insights and their ramifications. Richard Dawkins and Daniel Dennett are two who are constantly banging this drum. Would you talk a little bit about the way in which Christianity and evolutionary theory can fit together? Both Christianity and evolutionary biology pose very specific, but rather different, pictures of how the world is structured.

AYALA: I think it is a practical mistake for religious people, for Christians, to see science as a crutch or an apology, or a foundation for religion. I think that is ultimately damaging to religion. Some theologians and people of faith have tried to use scientific arguments to prove the existence of God. More often yet, some use current unknowns about the world and its origins as evidence of God's existence. I am persuaded very strongly that this is a mistake from the point of view of religion. It is the God of the Gaps approach to justify religious beliefs. There are events in the world whose causes we don't know and they conclude that therefore we can only attribute them to God. Science can, in principle, provide a complete view of nature, within its own sphere. The God of the Gaps approach leads to a continuous retreat as more and more natural phenomena become explained by science. And this reduces the credibility of religion in the eyes of many.

I once presented a paper in which I argued that the vision that emanates from Darwin completes the Copernican revolution. Physical science had provided a way of understanding the material world according to scientific principles, that is, a view of the physical world as matter in motion, where natural phenomena can be explained when the appropriate causes are known. Now, what the Copernican revolution had left out was an explanation of the origin and diversity of organisms, particularly their "design." There can be no doubt that an eye is made to see and a hand is made for grasping. So in the early nineteenth century, in England in particular, there were written the so-called Bridgewater Treatises, and also a book, *Natural Theology*, by the famous theologian William Paley, who also was a good naturalist. These books argued that the existence of design in living things proved that there was a Designer. Well, Darwin did away with that. Darwin made it possible to see the "design" of organisms as a consequence of a natural process – natural selection. And in that sense, he completed the Copernican revolution by making it possible to see everything in the world of nature as the consequence of natural processes and thus subject for scientific analysis.

There are recent versions of the God of the Gaps approach. Some theologians and philosophers say – and I'm including some people I very much respect – that in Heisenberg's indeterminacy principle one may see a little corner for divine action, for God to enter the world. I frankly think this is a categorical mistake, to see evidence of God in a particular equation – which only says that the product of two numbers expressing the precision with which we can measure two variables, position and momentum, is a constant; from which it follows that as one variable becomes very precisely known, the other variable becomes less and less well known, more uncertain.

SLACK: A retreat to God in the shrinking Gaps?

AYALA: Yes, absolutely. What if tomorrow some physicist finds out that Heisenberg's indeterminacy principle actually can be done away with? Say a deterministic explanation is found. Would we then reject the presence of God in the world? I don't want to underestimate the intelligence of people who think differently, but in my view science can now approach the entire natural world, and seek to describe it with the methods of science. But the questions that science asks are not the only questions of interest in trying to understand the world.

Let me return to imaginative literature and the arts. They are completely outside of the scientific realm. Artistic experience is outside the way of knowing that science represents. And yet the arts are a valid way of acquiring knowledge. Not just a valid kind of experience, but actually a valid way of acquiring knowledge. Shakespeare has a lot to say about human nature and our place in the world. This is knowledge, but it is not science. It is a different kind of knowledge. But it is valid. It is meaningful.

Trying to apply scientific standards to Shakespeare would be silly. It would be making what philosophers call a category mistake. Say that in a sonnet Shakespeare refers to his beloved as a rose. A scientist could say, "This guy is an idiot. A woman is not a rose." Of course the idiot would be the one who made that comment. Of course Shakespeare knows she is not a rose! But that doesn't mean that a man describing his beloved as a rose is not telling the world something meaningful about her, about his feelings, and about what love is like.

In this context, one of my favorite examples is *Guernica*, the famous painting by Picasso. One could describe the pigments, the canvas, the dimensions, the configuration of the images and so on. One could give a complete physical description of the painting, but still not have begun to tell us anything about what is important about the painting: the aesthetic experience, the message it conveys about human nature. Picasso had been commissioned by the Spanish Republican government to paint a large mural for a world exhibit in Paris. It was in April 1937, during the Spanish Civil War. The city of Guernica was completely erased by massive bombing by Nazi airplanes. It was the first time in history that a civilian population was completely destroyed from the air. The Germans were supporting Franco and they were trying out this modern form of warfare on the small town of Guernica. When Picasso heard about the bombing, he went into a fit of creative fury and sketched the huge painting (26'x12') in just a few days. Now, this historical circumstance is also something interesting to know about this painting, because it adds to its meaning and to the aesthetic experience. The meaning that *Guernica* conveys about human nature, about man's inhumanity to man, is completely outside the physical description of the painting.

My point is that the scientific description and understanding of the world tell something that is very valid and very important, especially for its technological and economic consequences. But in terms of fulfilling the human spirit, there is a lot to be said about the world – whether it is the physical world or the living world – which remains outside the realm of science.

So, back to your question: I see religion and science as addressing different realms of human experience. Religious experience gives us a different way of knowing, a different kind of knowledge, just as artistic experience gives us a different kind of knowledge.

SLACK: Would you describe it as two different ways of knowing a single truth? Or are the truths that we strive to access through science and through religion different in nature?

AYALA: I think these are semantic distinctions. A scientific and a religious view of the world do not overlap, but they concern different sources of knowledge. But I don't believe that they can be contradictory, that one can say that something is white and the other one say that that something is not white. They are just dealing with different dimensions of reality, different levels of experience.

They are views orthogonal to each other. They operate in different dimensions. They should be compatible, but, whether one calls them one truth and one world or many truths and many worlds, to me, is just semantic.

SLACK: There are areas where many people believe science and religion chafe. Biologists often object to the purposefulness Christianity ascribes to human life, and to the rest of the natural world for that matter. The most reductionist geneticists view life as not being purposeful in any grand sense, but being the product of the repeated application of an algorithm. And I know that the chafing between these two views causes a lot of people—

AYALA: Well, you have raised so many issues! First let me say in passing that precisely because of what you have said about purpose, I want to state that one issue that has interested me for more than twenty-five years is to explore philosophically and scientifically the meaning of the terms "purpose" and "teleology," and the roles that teleological explanations play in understanding evolution and organisms.

I would argue that evolutionary biology calls – but, of course, not only – for teleological explanations. Some forms of teleological explanations are scientific explanations. Anybody who thinks that everything in the world can be explained in a reductionistic way is just naive, even if he or she might be a very profound thinker, which individual reductionists often are. What I mean is that in order to understand the vertebrate eye we need to understand the function it serves – seeing – and also that it came into existence through a long evolutionary process precisely because it serves for seeing and seeing was helpful to organisms in survival and reproduction. We can take advantage of the seasons to grow crops, but the seasons did not come about because of this use, they are a consequence of the earth revolving around the sun. But eyes with their complex organization would never have come to be if it were not for the function they serve. This is a teleological explanation.

Not long ago I published a review in *Science* of the last book, *The Demon Haunted World*, by the late Carl Sagan. He was a very distinguished scientist and educator. Much of the book is very good. It deals critically with pseudo-science and anti-science. But when Sagan tries to explain what science is, he takes such a simple-minded, reductionistic approach that one can only be shocked. He says, for example, that, because the discovery of the structure of DNA showed that heredity is carried in the sequence of the nucleotides of DNA, biology has been reduced to the laws of physics and chemistry. So, he says, now everything can be explained by the laws of physics and chemistry. Well, I said in the review that that kind of "reductionism" is false; the reduction of biology to the laws of physics and chemistry is not possible. Let anybody try to explain the origin of species, or language, or the evolution of humans with the laws of physics and chemistry. You cannot get very far.

SLACK: How about the laws of natural selection?

AYALA: If Dawkins thinks that natural selection is sufficient to explain everything about the origin and make-up of organisms, I would say okay, at a certain level of the world, yes, natural selection is very powerful. But how do I explain language, or, for that matter, thought and so many other things – artistic experience – in terms of differences in reproductive success, which is what natural selection is. That is not to say that one has to imagine that there are some little spirits or extra things floating around inside humans. One doesn't need to claim that there are other entities (objects) besides those that are the subject of science. But there are different ways to understand reality. This relates to the one truth, many truths question that you raised before.

How can one explain freedom in terms of the laws of physics or the laws of biology? Now Sagan or Dawkins might say that we will be able to do this in the future. Well, that's hardly a scientific response. That is an act of faith.

SLACK: Aren't you posing a kind of God in the Gaps argument, where the gap is the unexplained area between different levels of scientific description, say, between physics and biology?

AYALA: No. That's not the same as the God of the Gaps. It's an argument for different levels of knowledge and of experience, and these can be justified in other ways as well. In any case, a reductionist answer is not justified at present even within the realm of science, because there are so many things about organisms that cannot be fully explained by the laws of physics and chemistry.

SLACK: Dawkins also claims that the kind of metaphors employed in religious thinking and religious description are intellectual hurdles in taking Darwinian theory to heart.

AYALA: I think this kind of attitude is as unfortunate as the one taken by religious people who think that science is in religion's way. We go back to the beginning of this conversation. Much of my interest in trying to work out the relationship between religion and science has to do with removing the obstacles before those people for whom religion plays an important role. And there are more of them than there are scientists. I want them to understand that science is not in the way of their religion. And then one hopes also to persuade some reluctant scientists that religion doesn't need to be in their way either.

A few months ago, the governing council of the National Academy of Sciences acknowledged a renaissance of attacks against the teaching of science in the schools on fundamentalist religious grounds and decided to act in various ways to protect that teaching, while acknowledging that science and religion belong to different realms of human activity. This had already been stated by the Academy some years earlier. I had been very involved in the early eighties at the National Academy of Sciences in dealing with these attacks against science and the teaching of science, specifically of evolution, in the schools. The National Academy of Sciences produced a booklet that eventually was used as part of an amicus brief presented to the Supreme Court of the United States. This booklet, which I mostly drafted, was also distributed in the schools and used in many other ways. But at that time some members of the Academy were not completely sure that the Academy should get involved with the issue of teaching science in the schools. I remember a conversation with the newly elected president of the National Academy, Frank Press, about this. This was 1980 or 1981. He was asking me, rhetorically, I suppose, in a private meeting, whether I thought the National Academy of Sciences should get involved. I said yes, I thought it should, because what was at stake was not the teaching of a particular scientific discipline, evolution, but rather survival of rationality in this country. If we allowed the Book of Genesis to be taught as science, as the state of Arkansas had legislated, this would be as bad for science as it would be for religion. Many religious authorities agreed. Incidentally, when the trial – *McLean* vs *Arkansas Board of Education* – took place in Little Rock – where Stephen Gould and myself and a couple of others were witnesses as scientific experts, among the plaintiffs who had initiated the lawsuit against the state of Arkansas were local bishops, the Methodist bishop, the Baptist bishop, the Catholic bishop, the Anglican bishop, as well as educational organizations and others. The booklet published in the early 1980s has now been revised and again published. I have played a role in preparing this 1999 revision of *Science and Creationism: A View from the National Academy of Sciences*, by chairing the committee in charge of it.

I believe that in the last few years we are entering a new era in the dialogue between science and religion. Rather than warfare we seek mutual respect and understanding.

SLACK: Or at least reconciliation.

AYALA: Yes, but more than reconciliation, mutual understanding. Moreover, the scientific and religious communities share some goals. We want the citizens of the United States, and of course the world, to live full lives and mature lives. Scientific literacy contributes to it, but there are other dimensions. The religious dimension is one.

Scientists should not be trying to make people religious, nor should ministers or theologians seek as a primary purpose to teach science. But many general goals are common to scientists and people of faith, such as improved education and a good life. We should work together towards those common goals, and for the rest, for the parts where our interests do not overlap, we should seek to make it clear they are not in opposition.

Unfortunately, there are scientists who think that there is conflict between science and religion. And there are religious people who think that the two are incompatible. Thus some Christian fundamentalists still want to see the Book of Genesis taught as if it were an elementary book of science. This is bad science. In my view, it is also harmful to religion.

2 Arno Penzias

The Elegant Universe

Arno Penzias shared the 1978 Nobel Prize in Physics for his part in the discovery of the first material evidence of the Big Bang. He and Robert Wilson detected a constant low-level noise with a super-sensitive horn antenna owned by their employer, Bell Labs. After repeatedly checking the device for defects and making sure the emissions weren't coming from the Milky Way, the Sun, or some other astronomical source, they realized that the "hum" must be background radiation remaining from the Big Bang.

Penzias has worked on a number of other historic projects, including Telstar and Echo, the first communication satellites sent into orbit by the United States. He became Bell Laboratory's Chief Scientist in 1995 and he remained with the company until 1998. He has more than a dozen patents to his name as well as twenty honorary degrees, over a hundred scientific papers, and he is the author of two books about technology's transformation of society. Today, Penzias works out of an office in his San Francisco home researching high-tech companies and directing venture capital toward them.

The practice of Judaism is more about behavior than it is about believing any particular thing, Penzias says. He resists the temptations to draw religious significance from his Big Bang work. "It just wouldn't be honest," he says. He has little patience for scientists who search for evidence of God in the world, or believe God is just beyond the horizon of their own field of study. It is precisely the elegant lack of God's fingerprints on the world that tell us most about the Creator, he implies. "You don't need somebody diddling around like Frank Morgan in the last scenes of the

Wizard of Oz to keep the world going. Instead, what you have is half a page of mathematics."

ARNO PENZIAS: First off, I'm Jewish. I was born in Germany, before World War II, into a family that was not terribly observant. I come from a Polish-Jewish heritage and all the uproar and dislocation that followed World War I and the beginnings of the Nazi era. Things were chaotic for us. Then we came to America, where I had a traditional Hebrew School education. In my more mature years, I've thought a bit more about religion, especially in regard to thinking about having children. Do I, for example, have a right to endanger my children by making them Jewish? Unlike someone who could become Presbyterian, say, where there is no risk involved, no pain involved, no downside, or at least not very much, with Judaism there is a tremendous problem of potential risk, which I have had to deal with. It is much more like the early Christian churches, where people who chose that faith did so in fear of their lives. Emotionally, I had that same kind of experience. So, with mixed feelings, I decided not only to remain overtly Jewish, but to make the world a little safer and more comfortable for other Jews by bearing witness, and at the same time also by making sure that my children experienced a Jewish upbringing.

GORDY SLACK: Would you say that your considerations were mostly ethical and cultural or that they were also fueled by a kind of a spiritual—?

PENZIAS: Very good question. I think they are more ethical and cultural than they really were fueled by any strong spiritual belief. Then, having gotten into this Big Bang cosmology in the early-mid 1960s, around the age of 30, I began to encounter some of the religious questions having to do with cosmology. I had to satisfy the questions reporters asked as well as my own questions on the subject. And over that period of time, I developed some views that have caused me to look at the relations between traditional religious teachings and my own experiences as a scientist. Like most scientists, I think, in the early stage I just did the work and didn't really question why I made the assumptions. You're just too busy. Since then,

I've become more philosophical about it. I've thought a little bit more about what science means. Having confronted people who don't think much of science, or who question it, in defending what I believe is a valid position I've had to rethink that position.

Science describes a branch of human knowledge. And knowledge is no more than an opinion, or a belief, at best, about how the world works. It's a limited set of observations that we try to make sense of. The scientific method has proven enormously valuable and has stood up against the test of opposition, so I think it's a very valuable way of thinking about the world. It isn't the only way to think about the world, and it's limited to a certain kind of knowledge and data and experience. It's the way I happen to think about the world. But there are others.

SLACK: Would you say that the world that science describes is the same world religion describes? Are they two means of approaching the same thing?

PENZIAS: No, they're quite different. I think religion does something more. Religion goes outside the world. Science can't. When religion tries to describe the world it gets into trouble. To the extent that religious thinkers are and ought to be interested in descriptions of the world, they are more customers for that information, questioners of it rather than creators of it – although every human being participates in the process of adding, hopefully positively, to the fund of human awareness. But that's not the main business of religion, nor should description of the world necessarily come from religion.

Occasionally, when religious belief comes in conflict with scientific or objective descriptions, people with religious beliefs have a perfect right to reject the scientific model, and say it's just wrong. The best example of that is Maimonides, who had the temerity to take on Aristotle in the twelfth century. In fact he was the first of the medieval thinkers who was willing to say that Aristotle might not be right. Aristotle preached, among other things, the eternity of matter. Maimonides's religious conviction told him that this is a purposeful world, and that a purposeful world can't be eternal, and therefore matter isn't eternal. He says, "In these matters, take no notion of the word of any man for the foundation of our faith that God created the world from nothing, that time did not exist before because it depends on the motion of the sphere that, too, was created." So we have matter, time and space being created out of nothing, which fits general relativity a lot better than Aristotle does. But whether it is right or wrong, the point was that this was his belief, and therefore he rejected Aristotle's description of the world. It's perfectly valid and important for religious people to look at the prevailing picture of the world, and when it doesn't match their belief system, they are in fact entitled to reject it.

The basis of religion, then, is not just in setting out and describing the world. That is a poor use of religion. I don't find much value in a microscopic religion which sees each tree controlled by its own minor deity. I think the primary modern religions put the world in context and so have to stand outside the world. Religion overshadows science because presumably it has a larger view. In the case of Maimonides, the purposeful, religious world rejected something that was scientific dogma for many centuries.

SLACK: But weren't Maimonides and Aristotle talking about the same world? There's a factual dispute.

PENZIAS: Sure, but the point is that Aristotle's came on observational grounds. Maimonides' came on religious grounds.

SLACK: Right, but they were talking about the same object.

PENZIAS: Of course. They both describe the world, but for two different reasons. Aristotle says, "I am an observer." Maimonides is not as good an observer. He's saying something about the foundation of our faith, which comes outside the world. He's taking the religious authority that goes beyond the world.

SLACK: Right.

PENZIAS: You used an interesting word there. "Right." Now, there's "right" that we can see as probably correct within the axioms of number theory or something. But then there's something else called "right," and "wrong," which plainly transcend the world. Now sociologists will say that "right" is a subject defined by a majority vote in some society. That's a different point of view. From the scientific point of view, "right" and "wrong" have no meaning other than "probably correct according to some axiom." From a theological point of view "right" and "wrong" are things that transcend the world. And so other views like those are of a purposeful nature. God, or however you describe it, then has some kind of seniority, or at least has a more important hold on one's world view than the mere description within the closed set. Because that set in itself can't be both complete and consistent.

SLACK: Let's talk for a moment about purposefulness. Is the fact that the world has purpose something you come to as a religious Jew, or is it a given about the world? Or is it a testable—?

PENZIAS: Faith is not testable. Logic only goes so far. Go back to Godel's hypothesis. As I said earlier, results that come from logical arguments ultimately have to be based on axioms that are either incomplete or inconsistent. Therefore science is always an incomplete description of the world. If one were to try to add something, whatever one tries to prove, you still know that you're going to have an incomplete system. It's incomplete for a lot of reasons. It's incomplete because we live finite human existences and we only have a finite amount of data. So we're never going to get complete knowledge of anything. We can get some very powerful descriptions. I urge you not to run into a lamp post when you get out of here, although I can't prove that it's going to hurt you. We're using inductive reasoning and so maybe this same kind of induction – maybe it's instinct, or maybe the echoes of the worlds which lie in our own souls – causes us to either believe in, or maybe to hope for, meaning and purpose, and right and wrong beyond that.

SLACK: How related are those two approaches to purposefulness; that is, "hoping for" and "believing in"? Is there a causal relationship?

PENZIAS: Sure, I think so. I think hope and belief always overlap to some degree. The best of scientists always struggle with their hopes. We put dignified words on it; we say that scientists must do double blind, that whenever they make observations scientists go to great lengths to make sure that they don't influence the outcome. There are so many experiments where people seem to have done a very careful job and seem to have been dispassionate, and then their own prejudice gets in there anyway. In something as cut and dried as deciding how much the fog weighs, or whatever, it's impossible to separate belief from wish or hope, desire, prejudice or point of view. By extension, I would argue that belief always has hope, or fear, which is the inverse of hope, associated with it.

SLACK: Do you think that this modern preoccupation with the universe as a meaningless place is a result of an over-application of the scientific practice of subtracting your hopes from your experiment? Some people, some scientists in particular, seem determined to prove – or at least to convince their colleagues – that the world is not inherently meaningful.

PENZIAS: Well, yes. Sure, I think that's fair. I don't want to speak about any individual's work. I know that there are many, many people who have a great emotional stake in a meaningless universe. And I can think of reasons why they might. But whether they are right or wrong is very hard to know.

One can look at it on psychological grounds. I don't think it matters. But certainly people can argue. In *Catch 22* Mrs Scheisskopf objects strongly when the hero says something about God being a jerk, or having a sense of humor, or some such thing. She says, "No, no. Don't say that!" He says, "Why? You don't believe in God." And she says, "Sure, I don't believe in God, but the God I don't believe in is a kind and loving father."

So we have our own belief systems. Part of it comes from not only over-reaction, but also the extent to which our point of view in one area has to go somewhere else. There is a desire for consistency. Science is a great part of the world and I don't wish to demean it. It's what I do for a living and I certainly use the scientific method every day of my life, whether I'm looking for the leak in the window behind you, or trying to publish a paper, or doing my income tax. I don't behave as if gremlins exist in the world. Although sometimes I have to remind myself of that. Sometimes I think the piece of paper I've lost must have disappeared even though I know that it profits no one to think of evil spirits under those circumstances.

To some extent, though, we all believe a little in magic. Our first experiences as sentient beings have magic associated with them. Children have this amazing power over the world. They just say, "I'm hungry," and they get fed. They say, "I'm wet," they get dried. All they have to do is say, "I feel lonely," and some powerful beings arrive and they hold them. Maybe this early magic is something that stays with people for a long time. We all have to overcome it as adults. Magic doesn't work. In the real world it's called adult responsibility and we get it at age two. Maybe that's why we're so mean to our parents at that time. You grow out of it and you say, "I don't believe in magic any more." But our belief in magic is very deep, and we have to work very hard to overcome it. And I even have to overcome it sometimes looking for a piece of paper. I can understand why some people, having struggled with their demons so much – sort of like being a reformed smoker – want to fight it in others as well.

The other thing is less psychological. It's just habit. I don't know if you know anybody who builds and frames houses. But a builder, framing houses, leaves the house every day and spends the entire day working under the assumption that the Earth is flat. He's not really on a round planet because as far as he is concerned, vertical is parallel, which it isn't. Vertical is parallel only on a flat Earth, not on a round Earth. So he takes his level and puts it on one two-by-four and another two-by-four. But coming home at night and looking at television, he sees a shot from space of this round Earth. But I don't think he makes the connection. But the question is, if I look down on the Earth from these asteroids, how can I use a level on a house? Well, that's a stretch. While the two are contradictory, I don't think many carpenters watching a space shuttle mission think about it.

The point is, scientists, at great emotional cost to themselves, usually work all day in meaninglessness. And then they come home and somebody says "meaning." It's tough. I hypothesize that that's one reason for what you're talking about.

SLACK: Do you feel like meaning and purpose are things you reflexively subtract when doing research?

PENZIAS: Just like the carpenter with the level, hardly anybody thinks about it. It's hard to believe. I think there has been kind of an inverse snobbery. Stephen Hawking, for one example, used this as a catchy way of ending his book, talking about the mind of God. But what others have done is to put God back into their work, which is to say that scientists then not only want to think of their system as consistent and valid, they want to think of it as complete. And so therefore as far in their work as they can see, which is never to the end, their furthest horizon, they then describe as God. The most interesting thing they've been working on lately becomes God. "If I look at these particles, or this particular area, if I understand how the galaxy works or why pigs oink, or some other fundamental question, now I've got the mind of God." Well, maybe.

SLACK: For cosmologists and astronomers it seems to be the most distant thing and for biologists it seems to be the smallest thing.

PENZIAS: Or the most organized thing. There is a well-known habit of human beings to rely on metaphor. Back to infantile things, we use our bodies as metaphors for the rest of the world. I once made a list of how many things have heads: pins, classes, beers, organizations, rivers. The list is enormous. And so we take our technology in metaphor. When the early Vikings had forges in the early Iron Age, all of a sudden gods of thunder had a hammer. The Mayans built their creation myths out of carvings. The Babylonians built creation myths out of mud. In the Middle Ages you see anatomy pictures with these little alchemists and devils going up ladders in these furnaces and smelting stuff and bellows and so forth. It looked like Renaissance technology or medieval technology. The nineteenth century did the same with hydraulic stuff. In the early twentieth century electricity was superlife: Frankenstein and Wolfman turning into one another with lightning. It goes on and on. Nowadays, it's computers. We extend ourselves as kind of a metaphor and we say what we know is everything. It's no different from the joke about the

New York taxi driver. "What do you have to know to be a taxi driver?" The answer: "Everything." Or a bouncer, or whatever kind of work or job it is. An actress, Molly Picon, once did a little song about how an actress has to know everything. Scientists have to know everything in the extreme. So they say, "If God exists He's right at the edge of my work."

I have no problem with scientists saying there is no God. But for them to say, "This is God," annoys me. It is blasphemy. It annoys me because they're misusing the word, which is at the very least disrespectful. They haven't got a clue what God is.

SLACK: It may be a way of handling their own hope and integrating the hope that moves us toward—

PENZIAS: Nothing there. It demeans the notion. They don't want to say there's no God. I have no problem with stretching the concept. But I have little patience for this misuse of one of the fundamental concepts of humankind in this absurd way.

SLACK: That fundamental concept, God, has been stretched every which way for a long time hasn't it?

PENZIAS: Well, I think there is an underlying truth, which is that there are different aspects. One of my favorite examples is Kepler going back beyond the Greeks in the Protestant Reformation. He was very ardently religious and studied theology and was essentially laid off, or given, in organizational terms, what one calls a lateral transfer. His seminary sent him off to a math job because they didn't want him there. He was a little too much of a fanatic for them. But there he was and he took this same religious belief into his own work and he said, "God is a law giver. God is trying to do this with simple, powerful laws." And so he worked with these various geometric figures to try to understand the planets. And he just assumed there was a simple law underneath it and he finally came up with his laws of motion. He tried some other stuff first, but his view of God was as the lawgiver.

Some people see God as a personal intervener in the world. I have a lot more trouble with others. The God of judgment, perhaps. I don't think they've been stretched. I think there are people who have different views on just what attribute they want to consider.

SLACK: Even within traditional Jewish theology there's a wide range of foci, and isn't some of it something like the scientific speculation about God occupying the margins of the universe?

PENZIAS: What do you have in mind, specifically?

SLACK: I'm thinking about the Jewish mystical tradition.

PENZIAS: Well, this is more the God of magic. This is why there is such resistance to that kind of mysticism in the Bible. It gets into magic and is intervening in a funny kind of way. If you say you can get the right set of letters and get something to happen, it's bringing magic in a way that is different from the view of the perfect creator. If you believe in an all-powerful creator, in some sense, an all-powerful creator can be inconsistent. The argument against my argument is of course, if He's all-powerful, is He consistent? If you think God is all-powerful and His Works are perfect, unimprovable, then why would you have somebody who can diddle around? In a perfect creation whatever is going to happen is inherent in the system and there is nothing to be fixed, nothing to be repaired.

Then of course you have the problem of whether there is such a thing as free will. Well, free will allows you to work in the world as it exists, not the modified world. That is, if you are within the rules. Within the rules, you are given great flexibility, great opportunities for good and evil. But you're not able to change the rules.

Of course, sometimes God does change the path of creation. If one believes some other traditions, it seems that God changes the rules and intervenes, such as when He spoke to Moses.

SLACK: I was talking to a Jewish molecular biologist at Berkeley a few weeks ago, and he was saying that as his religious understanding has progressed, he's gained a higher tolerance for paradox. And he quoted Rabbi Akiva as saying, "All is foreseen and free will is given." I think he's suggesting that free will is one of the elements of God's world, and it can't be undone any more than any of the other laws. And I guess that does point eventually to a paradox which this biologist, anyway, says must be tolerated.

PENZIAS: Well, it is a paradox and you can tolerate it or not. That is, one does get to these questions of uncertainty. There is a limit. If you look at the world of physics as we understand it, it is indeterminate. The world described by the laws of physics is unpredictable. We see that. This paradox, I think, at least for many people, had less meaning after quantum mechanics than before. If in fact the world is just a billiard ball place, then in fact everything is determinate. Under those circumstances, there is really no room for free will.

One of the remarkable things is that the more you study the world's details, the less meaning it seems to have. The world is unpredictable. And that's an observational fact. The unpredictability of the world is fundamental to the way the world behaves, which is to me remarkable.

Now, I can imagine building a classical world in which you would have a problem with free will because if you set it in motion everything would be predictable in advance.

SLACK: There's something that you said in an interview I read that reminded me of Wittgenstein, who said, "We feel that when all scientific questions have been answered, the problems of life remain completely unanswered." Do you find any truth in that statement?

PENZIAS: Well, science doesn't solve life's problems. It may provide description but it doesn't provide meaning. Sciences may provide some clues to meaning, but very weak ones. This is one of the reasons I specifically say we cannot know the mind of God. Because the meaning of the world, if any, is an issue which can't be described, could not be handled by a self-consistent physical description of the world.

The paleontologist Stephen Gould delights at taking apart nineteenth-century folks who drew homilies from scientific or observational facts. The kinds of things they said tended to be tendentious, and so in some sense what Gould says is quite right. The kinds of lessons that you draw from the physical world are suspect because they are not proofs. You can pick anything out and make it a homily. But the answer to your question is that the meaning of life isn't in science. The meaning of life has little to do with how good our description of the world is. The description of the world we have today is remarkable in its abilities. I think that very few lay people have the remotest understanding of the deep level of interconnection existing in the picture of the world we have. That is, the same laws of mechanics which guide the planets, appropriately modified and added to quantum mechanics, are able to explain why the poison of certain vipers in Sumatra behave in ways which are similar to nicotine. You have to look at the details of molecules. We can talk about the proteins on the surface of an AIDS virus – just minute, detailed, wonderful understandings. We have all this. We understand atoms; we understand disease. We can tell the chemical composition of galaxies three-quarters of the way across the universe. And yet, people can still read the Book of Ecclesiastes and it's very hard to tell that from something a very thoughtful Berkeley professor might have written. So that's a really good support for this argument. With all of this scientific progress we've made, the addition to our understanding of meaning is not all that hot. It's a fair assumption that it has been somewhat improved, but it certainly hasn't been revolutionized. And so I think it's fair to say religion and science describe two different things.

SLACK: Would you say, as a scientist who is also somewhat religious, that as you have made progress in your own scientific understanding of the world and the universe, that there has also been progress in your spiritual life?

PENZIAS: I have no way of knowing.

SLACK: But you don't experience that connection?

PENZIAS: I don't experience it in that sense. What is happening is that I am getting older. In 1964 my third child was born and that was the year we blundered onto the background radiation. The birth of a child probably has, in the long term, a much bigger effect. Things like being sick, losing my parents, all sorts of things. Life goes on. You live life every day. Thinking now of this world where technology and the fruits of science have become so important, has called science into question. We have to talk about belief systems, and for various reasons. The fact that one can talk about these things as a scientist probably hasn't sharpened my beliefs. But in terms of what I've discovered or not discovered as a human being has a lot to do with it. Which is to say in the small, the thing I already said in the large: progress in the understanding of the physical world doesn't change it. I think that's consistent.

SLACK: I have talked to a number of scientists in this project who feel there is an intimate relationship between the progress that they make as scientists and the progress that they make as religious people.

PENZIAS: I wonder how they separate out the effects of growing older and growing professionally, say professional progress and personal progress. Maybe. If it works for them, fine. I'm not knocking it. I don't think I've experienced it in my own life.

SLACK: From the outside, it is very tempting say that spiritual and scientific breakthrough would be related in your case because it is so tempting to relate your discovery of background radiation, of the Big Bang, to something about God.

PENZIAS: It is tempting, but it wouldn't be honest.

SLACK: Let's talk for a minute about technology and the metaphors that are now borrowed from computers and how those are woven into our understanding of what it is to be a human being and what it is to be a spiritual human being.

PENZIAS: What I look at in my book about computers and the idea of information is the difference, in a very mechanical way, between the ways human beings and machines solve problems. Essentially a computer is merely a pocket calculator that can push its own buttons and remember what it's done. So all it's doing is mathematical operations and the only knowledge it has in the mathematical sense is the numbers in its registers. Any meaning or connection with the rest of the world has to be applied in one of two ways: either through a sensor, or, by somebody in the outside world who associates some meaning to the numbers. You could decide, for example, this number is population or this information is about Fred. And that's because you use a translation of numbers to say that the number seventeen with something around it means something specific. But all the computer has stored in it is numbers. So, while one set of numbers can point to another set, you don't have any outside information.

It's like a dictionary. When I first came to the United States, I was floored by something here which I hadn't realized existed: a dictionary that has only one language. I could understand the concept of a dictionary, which was to take German words and put them into English and vice versa. But here was a dictionary in only one language. I could not understand how you could have such a thing. And, of course, everyone else thought I was stupid. But it's a fundamental question: how can a dictionary do you any good? It's because the person reading it has some notion of words that are not themselves the words that would also need to be looked up. Otherwise, there's nothing there. It's all referential. The computer only has look-up tables. A look-up table is some number that is again connected to the real world. That doesn't give you a lot.

It's a limited thing. Whether it's a distributor computer or nowadays a network, or web, or whatever, people want whatever is the latest enthusiasm. I don't think it's any better than Frankenstein and Wolfman and electricity. It comes from the same genre; why should we be right this time? We're always infatuated with our latest discovery.

But another of the great miracles of human beings is the ability to scale. That is, we always take whatever the problem is and our brains rescale it. Whatever size problem we have that day looks to us to be everything.

Imagine I'm in this cave and I've got a club. If I put on my bearskin and go away from the fire, there are a hundred million saber-toothed tigers out there. Sooner or later, I'm going to get eaten and my kid is going to get eaten. How then can I possibly go out there? Well, you say, sooner or later you have to go out. You'll deal with it. You think about a much smaller part of the world. You don't worry about the fact that the Arctic ice is that way and some burning desert that way. You just deal with your little part of the world. We all tend to do that, and it's quite useful. If we didn't do it, we wouldn't get out of bed in the morning. It's as useful as thinking the world is flat when you do carpentry. It's not right. It doesn't make it right; the fact that it's useful doesn't make it right.

SLACK: It seems that what you did as the director of a lab and as a researcher yourself was wedded to a methodology that depends essentially on finding new ways to look at things.

PENZIAS: Within a framework. New ways within a certain framework, sure.

SLACK: Religion, on the other hand, seems to be oriented toward tradition, toward repeating things that have been done in the same way for a long time. I'm wondering if shifting back and forth between looking for something new and looking to something old is comfortable for you?

PENZIAS: Every religion is different. The point about Judaism is the lack of dogma. There are some things that you believe, but I don't worry about that much. I don't look at religion as something where I'm forced to believe dogma, where I'm forced to take things as given. There are certainly traditions. There are things that I wish were correct, things that help me understand the world. You're not always sure whether they're correct or not. That's a long-winded way of saying that I don't see religion as being that confining. Other people do. But again, I take it mostly from an ethical or cultural perspective. I don't spend a lot of time on questions of dogma. On the other hand, I think that the behaviors are certainly valuable.

SLACK: Which of the behaviors are left if you subtract the dogma?

PENZIAS: Judaism is a religion of action, not of belief. You can apply the following: ask a Jew, "Would you be willing to become a Christian?" And the typical answer is, "Well, what would I have to do?" On the other hand, ask a Christian, "Would you be willing to become a Jew?" and the answer is usually, "What do Jews believe?" Now, if you went to a Moslem, I think you would be much more likely again to talk about action. I think it has to do with geography, because Christianity has become a very much more Western religion. Just look at the Hebrew language: there's nothing there but verbs. So it's all action. On the other hand, an English telegram is perfectly understandable if you take all the verbs out. It's really based on a kind of objective reality system. It's different. Now, that's not to demean one or the other, it's just saying, I don't encounter a conflict in Judaism.

There are certain prayers we say we all believe. I remember the responsive English readings from the High Holidays that are something like, "We all believe His works are perfect." "We all believe this. We all believe that." You say this stuff. If I were really honest about it, I probably wouldn't say it, but since it's a part of— I say it without— I'm not really— Well, I know, it may be a bit of hypocrisy. But somehow you go along and you can't break everything down.

At the last place where I worked, a very kind, very gifted manager decided what we needed was a credo for our organization. And he said, "We believe the following things." You know, "We believe that the customer is the most important thing." I became very uncomfortable. I'm willing to say, "Our job is to act for customers." But to say, "We believe that nothing is as important as blah blah blah." Well, how does he know? I would have a hard time with that. I would have a hard time going into any situation that required that I have certain beliefs. On the other hand, saying that I hope there is a God is saying I hope there are some ultimate truths. I don't know exactly what they are. I have a list of what I'd like them to be. So the yearning for this, and in some sense perhaps working hard on articles of faith is a great thing. I can certainly see its value. It just doesn't happen to be something that I am practicing. Quite likely, if I'd been raised in another religion, I might find it more attractive. The short answer is that I don't think I have the problem.

SLACK: Harry Rubin, a molecular biologist at Berkeley, was friends with the physicist Walter Elsasser. The last thing Elsasser wrote to him was this: "I really think that all the noise-making that history is willing to exhibit is clearly one specific thing. Namely that the Creator wants to hide organic order wherever it goes beyond classical causality from the eyes of the observer." And Dr Rubin seemed to think that that was something, although Elsasser was not an observant Jew, that reflected a kind of a Jewish approach to interpreting God's role. I found that intriguing. God as an Obscurer as opposed to a Revealer of the underlying structure of the universe.

PENZIAS: Well, I don't see it that way. I would say it goes back to perfection. That is, if you look at these walls here, you don't see any saw marks. I think Jim Trefil, in one of his books, said something like, "If God created the universe, he would have done it elegantly." Elegance is the absence of the imprint. If we have a creation by an all-powerful Creator, the absence of the imprint of that creation is probably His greatest achievement. When you think about doing this whole thing, you don't need somebody diddling around like Frank Morgan in the last scenes of the *Wizard of Oz* to keep the thing going. Instead, what you have is half a page of mathematics, which does everything all the way up to the little repairers that go up the DNA ladders. It's all in there in a half a page of math. That's the difference. That's what's obscuring the purpose. It does look perfect. The fact that God is able to create these scientists who think that they know it all, who think there is no purpose at all, who say, "Look, it's all down here next to my theory," is one point of view. And there's the other point of view, which in Trefil was, "It's a lot harder to write the Constitution than the Federal Register." Look at how many words there are in the Constitution, as opposed to how many words there are in a bill to regulate the amount of margarine you're allowed to use under some circumstances, or oil depreciation or some damned thing. The point is, as people get less expert on these things, their own stuff follows them. So it's not God the Obscurer, it's the elegance of the Creator. In some sense, the power of the Creation lies in its modesty.

SLACK: And so modesty and elegance are related?

PENZIAS: In this case, modesty and elegance are related. There's no plaque on this thing, you know, "Built by the so and so." You go to the Parthenon and you look at this thing and there is no sign saying "Built by the Greeks."

3 John Rodwell
A Priest at Work

John Rodwell is a Professor of Plant Ecology at Lancaster University in England and a priest in the Anglican Church. Best known for coordinating the first systematic and comprehensive account of British vegetation, Rodwell's five-volume work, *British Plant Communities*, is used by all British land-management agencies and provides a common taxonomic language for government, business and environmental groups. As a botanist, it is the structure and function of vegetation types that currently hold his highest interest: their diversity, relationships to climate, soils, and human influences and conservation. The preservation of environmental resources is also a key theological concern of Rodwell's. What, he asks, are the ethical and spiritual implications of the human capacity for creativity and for the human proclivity for environmental destruction?

Rodwell likens the taxonomic work he does in botany to the blessings he conducts as a priest. Bestowing the proper names on both plant communities and the sacraments, he says, are ways of liberating them, of allowing them to express God's intentions more fully and of drawing out their inherent goodness. This is a fascinating and satisfying process, he says, but it can also be an agonizing one. For the grain to become bread, it must be crushed. As creation unfolds into its uncountable and stunning manifestations, it groans with the suffering and agony of transformation.

JOHN RODWELL: I'm a scientist by profession and I'm a priest. I've been ordained as an Anglican priest for twenty-one years or so. I never wanted to be any other sort of priest than a practicing scientist. I've always had a model of priesthood in which the ministry is kind of hidden within the work, or at least so intimately bound up with the work that it's difficult to disentangle a separate strand.

GORDY SLACK: You say that you see your scientific life and your religious one as intertwined, which still suggests that the threads have distinct identities.

RODWELL: Yes. I'm interested in the parallels between theological thinking and scientific discovery and methodology. What little I've contributed theologically has been mostly in this realm. I'm interested in scientific creativity and the creativity of God, so there's that intertwining.

I think, though, that there is a more profound relationship between what I do as a scientist and what I do as a priest. My science deals with the same stuff as my religion does. I don't make a separation between the material that I study as a scientist and the material with which I deal as a priest. I've thought quite a lot over the past twenty-one years about what it is that makes me a priest as opposed to a lay person. I think that most centrally it has to do with blessing – the discernment of an inherent goodness and dependency in creation. This is something that I find quite difficult to separate from my work as a scientist.

SLACK: You are a botanist. Would you describe yourself as a conservation biologist?

RODWELL: Yes, but that's not a term which is as current here in England as it would be in the United States. Technically, I'm a vegetation ecologist. My work is, in large measure, fairly straightforwardly descriptive because there's a long backlog of describing the natural world at a second- or third-order level of organization. We know a fair amount about species, but we still have a lot to learn descriptively about how species are put together in communities or ecosystems. In European terms, I'd be called a plant sociologist, or phytosociologist, or vegetation scientist. However, a great deal of what I do has importance in the realm of conservation because conservation is built upon accurate knowledge of resources, and also on some understanding of how realistic it is to sustain them. A lot of my work is used directly for this purpose.

SLACK: When you say that your science deals with the same "stuff" as your religion, and when you talk about this notion of blessing, or the discernment of holiness, what springs to my mind is the deep-ecology notion of the intrinsic value of nature.

RODWELL: Yes, I think that is very important to me professionally. I would say it is valuable to me religiously, theologically and also in my spiritual life. But perhaps if I could go behind that, I'd talk about the importance of the simple existence of the stuff. It's rather hard to separate value from existence. It's a big philosophical problem, isn't it? I'm very interested in the fact that the stuff of creation is simply there. As Augustine would say, "God looks at it as His, but not Himself." There's a degree of possessiveness toward what's been made which makes it intrinsically valuable to God and to us. It is deeply interesting to think of something that has been called into being within a realm of freedom, which God has given it. I see my rather old-fashioned, essentially descriptive type of science as being intimately involved with the discovery and the celebration of that kind of extraordinary gift. A lot of what I do would be accurately described in that way. I describe plant communities that are, in a sense, artifacts. They are not arbitrary, but they're kind of abstractions at one level or another. I am very aware of a tension between my desire to impose my perception of order and my desire to allow things to be what they actually are. I would say that I am trying to discover the names that were given to the realm of Creation by God Himself. I am trying to liberate them, to allow them to be what God wanted them to be. That has partly to do with them and partly to do with me and the way in which humanity groans and travails its way toward understanding. I can't separate the process of understanding and the process of the things being themselves. Our understanding things is actually a part of their liberation, or at least it should be. St Francis preached to the birds that they should go away and sing in gratitude. I see science as being an articulation of the gratitude of Creation for its existence by a realm that cannot adequately speak for itself.

SLACK: I have never heard taxonomy or plant ecology described in anything like those terms before. I'm very interested in this idea of naming something as a devotional act, or as an act of elevating the thing named and bringing it closer to its true or complete potential. I like it a lot.

RODWELL: The most powerful analogy for me is the celebration of the Mass. Within half an hour I go from my desk at the university to the university chaplaincy. I spend my morning pronouncing over these botanical entities. I try to give them a shape, and to communicate to other people what they're like while doing justice to the fuzziness of the data. Then suddenly I am in front of two gifts of Creation, bread and wine, exercising a naming act, and saying, "This is the body of Christ." This is for me the most powerful kind of illumination of what I do in both my realms. It is also the most profound reminder of the responsibility and the burden of pain involved. To obtain the bread that is used in the liturgy, the grain is crushed – it offers itself up as it were – and then we eat it. You can't get much more basic than that. I think that's a very profound reminder of the theological importance of naming and setting things in a realm of signs. There is a Welsh artist named David Jones who wrote quite a lot about setting things in a context of signs. This is what he said art was about, and I think that's true of science too. It's a matter of putting information and beings in a realm of understanding that should be deeply perceptive of the struggle that Creation has to be itself, and of which we are an intimate part.

Over the twenty-one years I have been a priest, I have wondered from time to time, "What exactly is it that makes me a priest?" I think, actually, it is really only the liturgical act of blessing, in a sense, and the way in which I am able to exercise that blessing in my ordinary work. I think I would say that blessing is a declaration of the intrinsic goodness of things, that is: we belong here. We are at home in Creation; it is intrinsically good although it is very painful to liberate that goodness.

SLACK: Are there links between points of scientific discovery in your career and moments of religious discovery?

RODWELL: That's a difficult one because the realm that I work in as a scientist is one that does not have readily identifiable moments of discovery. It has moments of satisfaction that are perhaps all too easy. I am now working on the fifth volume of a series of books describing 295 British plant communities. They each have sub-types and I've written descriptions of each one of them. There can be a feeling at the end of a day of, "Wow! That's neat! I've really sewn that up." I think those are suspect moments because it may all be too neat.

My moments of theological discovery have actually been quite powerful but diffuse. They have often been filtered through personal pain in my own life or through discoveries about myself and about people I love, which are not very comfortable. Much of my theological insight has come from those difficult times – from the death of my parents and so on.

A common theme I could put my finger on here is yearning: the sense of the incompleteness of it all, the brokenness of the vision. The fact that although I've done certain things there is a vast territory left undone. Britain is so tiny. At the moment, I am working with a man from Novosibirsk. He has come here for a month with data from forests stretching seven thousand kilometers from the Ural to Vladivostok. This is on the kind of scale that, being from California, you would understand. But it is extraordinary for us. Britain is a very small country; about the size of North Carolina. It is extremely varied, but my realm is actually fairly trivial. It is sobering to note that my vision is very incomplete. There is a restlessness, a kind of yearning and a desire for completeness. There is a sense that although everything here was created good, it is very incomplete and longs for a kind of consummation. I would hope that my descriptive activity is part of the progress to that kind of completion. But because it is so broken and fragmentary, it is also part of the kind of awkward incompleteness of it all.

I do believe very strongly that this yearning of my own search for knowledge is divine. That sounds grandiose, but I would like to think it could be part of God's own yearning. The Epistle to the Romans, Chapter 8, I would think of as being a critical text in this respect: Creation is incomplete; it yearns for completion. But the yearning with which it yearns is actually God's yearning. He's the one who wants it to be complete. I'm not a strong supporter of Teilhard de Chardin's idea that creation is pulling toward a particular point, but I certainly feel it is pulling somewhere. Like Augustine's sense of homesickness, I think that's where the moments of discovery have come. Certainly, the moments of discovery about the incompleteness of vision in my science have been, I would hope, religious moments.

SLACK: I suppose there is a limit to completeness built in to the kind of work that you do. Certainly, working with plant or animal communities, there is a fuzziness that will never quite go away.

RODWELL: Yes, and of course there's a deep intellectual debate that has taken place over this. Much of this debate was stimulated in the States, between the two ecologists Clements and Gleason, about whether plant communities exist or if things are very individualistic. Certainly, there is a fuzziness about this second-order thing that is even worse than working with species. One needs an awareness of the sheer complexity of it. I am not a great purist taxonomically. There are people in the phytosociological world in Europe whose whole life is what would be called syntaxonomy. They work solely within a strict code of phytosociological nomenclature. The precise naming and authorizing of these communities is their whole life. I would say the world is too complex and life is too short to be too worried about that. What one wants is a set of working categories in order to be able to do something with them.

SLACK: Here, however, that kind of a decision may have very profound practical consequences. If something is designated a subspecies as opposed to a species, it may, or may not, receive some kind of legal protection. What is a deep philosophical debate has become a very real political debate: whether phylogenetics or communities or species ought to be the deciding characteristic in determining conservation values.

RODWELL: That's true at this level of communities too. I coordinated this work to describe the vegetation of Britain and it's become very much associated with my name because I'm editor of the books. It is now accepted as a standard tool by all the major agencies in Britain so everybody uses it. For example, the nuclear industry uses it to talk to nature conservation agencies, since they can both use the same language and the same terminology. I've seen these units, which to me are essentially descriptive, being translated into something with evaluative authority. What was for me a kind of descriptive norm has become a set of standards. If, for example, a particular field does not match up to a description of a traditional hay meadow, or a bit of forest isn't old growth as it has been described in the book, then individuals or agencies may say that it's not worth protecting. And this, as you've described, has become a problem. We're working quite hard to try to show that it shouldn't have that kind of authority.

SLACK: I suppose that is another way in which naming something reifies it, makes it more real.

RODWELL: Yes. Certainly to people who've come to regard the descriptions in the books, which are abstractions from data from many places, as the real thing. I'm involved at the university with groups of philosophers and this project has had a very diffuse and profound effect on the way in which these agencies work. Somebody told me I didn't know the language but I was describing the kinds of data that we've used, and these philosophers said, "Oh no, no. You think it's just about data but it's not. What your team has done is invent a form of knowledge." And I think, philosophically, that is what has happened. Within this frame, which is very creative and productive, you've also got this tendency to reify and authorize things according to how closely they match what's been described. Communities are a bit different from species in the sense that you might find an individual butterfly or bird, and you might photograph it or catch it or stuff it or pin it down, but with a community, the thing has a second order of variation that is rather elusive.

SLACK: But there is certainly a great temptation, despite its elusiveness, to call it quite real.

RODWELL: Yes, there is. I see that as an enormous tension. We've built a training program to teach people how to use this scheme. The mission statement of our training program is to give people the skills and confidence to use it. While believing that it's true and reliable to a degree which will enable them to do their work, enhance their own skills and deliver the goods that they are supposed to be paid to produce, we at the same time try to help them develop a degree of skepticism. It comes to a sharp focus, actually, in using particular tools. For example, we have some expert computer systems that people have written to enable people to input data from a site and obtain "an answer" about what kind of plant community it is. Consultants, particularly, are very keen on just using these computerized keys. You feed in the list of species and it says it's type "X" and they just write it down. But there is supposed to be a distance between the user and the scheme in which you negotiate a relationship, an understanding. We've had to work very hard to get people to do that.

SLACK: Perhaps there is a religious analogy, or a shared principle, here as well. Naming something also can separate you from it. It can be alienating, and as a taxonomist one must remind oneself that though you've got the name, that is quite distinct from the thing. You have to remind yourself to constantly go back and remember the thing in itself.

RODWELL: You're right. I think it's a tension – it's possessive on the one hand: "It's mine." Of course, taxonomists, even at the community level, many syntaxonomists in Europe like syntaxonomy because they can invent a community and they can get their name on it and the date, as with a species. That's one thing, yes. And then there is this kind of, "There it is and here I am. It's mine." I think we should, as religious people, return to the relationship between God and His Creation to understand the proper sense in which He makes room. I have a very primitive, visual sort of mind and I quite like Jurgen Moltmann's view of the kind of medieval Jewish mysticism, of God breathing in: *tzimtzum*. He breathes in, and when He has breathed in, then there is room for something that is not Himself, but which is His. I think that's the space in which Creation exists. It's that relationship of intense love and concern and that tension between liberation and possessiveness that I think should be at the heart of what science and other creative activities are about.

Another aspect of my own interest and understanding of this is that there's not a sharp line between science and, say, painting, or even making a pie, or other creative activities. You have the same tension between ownership and liberation. And I don't see science as being characterized by, say, rationality and art as being characterized by something else. They're all characterized by imagination. That is a very important principle. It's an issue on which I disagree with John Polkinghorne, for example, with whom I've had this out from time to time. He is more interested in rationality, I think, and I am more interested in imagination. I see imagination as being a Divine principle. I guess if I were preaching now, using that kind of language, I would even be rash enough to say God conjures up these things. It's like magic, almost: poof! He conjures them out of nothing. That seems quite magical, and not having to do with rationality. I think there should be an element of that in science. It makes it sound mystical, but I don't mean that.

SLACK: Let me invoke another countryman of yours who would certainly disagree with you, and that is the geneticist Richard Dawkins. He feels that religious thinking obscures many of Darwin's primary insights. Would you talk a little bit about the fit between Christianity and evolutionary thinking and its applications in systematics and in botany?

RODWELL: Yes. Though it's not a realm in which I am an expert, one thing I would say to start with is that I regard Darwinism, or evolutionary theory, as a set of myths. I think it's a set of complex, related ideas and principles that help us make sense of the natural world. I think there is something profound about it, in the sense that it communicates some truth. But I don't see evolutionary theory as being very neat; it leaves a lot to be explained. I should add that the explanatory power of evolutionary theory is not something I spend very much time thinking about. I invoke it in lectures; it's obviously something I take for granted in the way I talk about things. I'm not a believer in any of the major alternatives – the fundamentalist view of Creation and so on.

I'm sympathetic to Dawkins in the sense that I'm not in favor of invoking divine explanations when the others run out. I don't want to do that. And yet, there is certainly a realm in which I don't find the severe rationalism of somebody like Dawkins very powerful. An example I've used before is Maximilian Kolbe in Auschwitz. He volunteered to be starved to death in place of another person who had a family. I can't see science, or Dawkins, or rationality, or evolution helping me very much there. That is not the package of explanations I find myself calling upon then – not that I have *any* to call upon at such moments, except a profound kind of silence and reflectiveness, a sort of agony. But what's left over, after the rational explanations, is some anxiety about calling actions like this wasteful or pointless. They do seem to me to have some meaning.

SLACK: Would you please talk a little bit about the sense of purpose, or directionality, which Christianity assumes in its interpretation of human life and the unfolding of the universe? Is this at odds with an assumed lack of purpose in a strict application of the scientific method?

RODWELL: I don't find ideas of direction or *telos*, in that kind of pointy way, very convincing or helpful; this idea that things are moving to a single kind of focus, or point of completion, or end. I see end in the sense of telos as being that the end of man is to glorify God and praise Him forever.

SLACK: You interpret "purpose" in terms of "meaning" as opposed to "ending point."

RODWELL: Yes, I think so. Yearning. I come back to this question of *apokaradokia*, as it would be in St Paul's Greek. Yearning and groaning, the kind of inability to swallow because you're so full of some kind of lump of awkward unresolvedness of things. That's the kind of incoherence about the yearning of Creation that I think is not inexplicable. There's a pattern to Creation. It is scientifically describable and we don't need to invoke a kind of "wind up the watch and see the watch working" and think, "Fantastic. God has made this." I think it's much more complicated than that. Dawkins is right in that respect. It's too painful, too incoherent, too messy to have that degree of persuasiveness. For example, descriptively, looking at it and thinking, "Gee, that pattern is fantastic, isn't it? Nobody but a Creator could have made that." There's a good deal more pain and awkwardness about the way things work. For example, animals killing their own young, and the ruinous kind of waste of the whole thing. It doesn't make sense as being entirely benign. But at the same time, I think the very incoherence of the yearning is extremely important. It is looking for somewhere to go. I don't think there is a single place for it to go, but it's wandering around in a way that I guess evolution would describe to some degree. It's going in a particular direction; there is not a single focus of its end, but it is held within an overriding kind of concern. Let's put it this way: the idea of *tzimtzum*, you know, God breathes in. He breathes in from a space He previously occupied; that is, there is an outer horizon of His concern. Everything that exists is within this space – nothing is outside His realm of concern. It is held within a free space. It develops in a way that is painful and has its own momentum. It is still somehow within His frame of Love. The outer boundary of all this is defined by Him and what He is like. However, within this there is a great deal of room for all that is happening. What it draws on is God's original intention for what it should be. I would say it is like having a child. The child begins to walk and you just put your hand under its bottom and back and you just push it away and say, "Go on then. Go on." Or perhaps you stand it at the other side of the room and sort of beckon to it. It sort of wobbles; and it's that imagery of loving concern. And that awkward— I don't know if you have children, but you have a partner, I think, because I spoke to her. A wife?

SLACK: Yes, my wife. And I do also have a son. Today is his first day at nursery school.

RODWELL: Ah, then there you are. I need say no more. There you are, you're sitting there and thinking, "My God, I wonder how he is. I'm sure he's okay, and I'd love to be there, but I must let him do it on his own." I would say, Gordy, that's exactly it.

Another crude model would be the artist struggling with his clay and thinking: "Oh, God, this is just not coming. Grrr. I can't make it work." And then he turns to go to the other side of the room to smoke a cigarette and sit and look at it and think, "How am I going to get this thing to actually be what I want it to be?" It's all of these things – letting go, moulding, having a try at making it work. That's the model. I think the limit of the horizon is God's own being and concern. The mystery I see as a priest and as a scientist is the relationship of ownership and freedom and liberation, the working out of the sheer ontological surprise that it's all here.

SLACK: From our point of view, as human parts of the Creation, there is big a question of what it means to be both owned and free.

RODWELL: Yes, and I think I would say humankind is in a profoundly privileged position in this respect. We are the creatures who can articulate the groaning of Creation. We are the only creatures who can sit here as we are now, talking across the Atlantic on a telephone about the rest of Creation. No other element of Creation can have this kind of conversation about itself, and this gives us a profound responsibility of understanding and stewardship.

SLACK: There are times when that ability makes us look a bit like adolescents. We are old enough to consider these things, but not mature enough to figure them out. It sometimes makes me yearn for the pre-language days of childhood before the alienation and responsibility introduced by self-consciousness.

RODWELL: It's true. A few years ago I went to the Normandy Beaches, where the invasions took place in the Second World War. My wife and I got on a bus, and sitting behind us on the bus was a young American guy, from "Dry Prong, Louisiana" – wonderful. "My daddy's the Chief of Police." Anyway, he was majoring in the D-Day landings in college and he said, "Can I come along with you folks? I don't know any French." So we went to the cemetery at Omaha. There are nine thousand tombs of American boys at this place and it's completely overwhelming. My wife and I were immensely moved because we're both children of the Second World War. This guy – I guess he was about twenty-one – just lay there on the grass with his Marlborough, and I thought, "Gosh, this guy is crass." And then I thought, "Now hang on, most of the guys under this soil are like him. They would not have been here had they not had that kind of brash lack of understanding and lack of concern." That was a real sobering moment. I was there in that cemetery, partly because of the sacrifice of these guys. It was a really profound moment. But, yes, you're right, I think there is a kind of awkwardness because we are new in Creation. I suppose that that is perhaps where the power of the evolutionary story is quite important. It locates us intimately as a part of the groaning.

SLACK: There seems to be a division, among the scientists I talk to, between the optimists and the pessimists, about the relationship between religion and science. What are your hopes and expectations about the next century? Do you think this is just a blip of cooperation we're seeing between scientific thinking people and religious thinking people?

RODWELL: That's an interesting question, and a difficult one. Perhaps I'd have to answer it in a number of ways. I'm not very optimistic about the Church's ability to take the world seriously, and that would include the natural world. A perpetual problem I have in dealing with my fellow priests and with the Church as an institution is that it seems to not be very interested in what the world is like. I'm hardly on the forefront of science in any important kind of way, but I am working on a little coalface; I'm describing things that have not been described before and making small discoveries. I can be watching this guy from Siberia with this piece of software working with the skills we've given him to map his seven thousand kilometers and thirty-one communities of forest. Nobody has done this before. It has all been one color on a map for three thousand kilometers and suddenly there are many colors and a lot of detail, and here he is conjuring this sort of intimate pattern and I think, "Gosh, that's fantastic. To see this man actually doing this, at this moment." So, there are modest kinds of discoveries of this sort. But I'm very conscious that the church is not really very interested in what I have to tell it about these discoveries. Of course, there is an intellectual problem in that not many religious people or fellow-priests would understand the terminology. I have to work hard to convert it into something interesting. But that's not really the problem. The problem, I think, is that there is a profound lack of awareness that the world is the substance of what religion is about. There is a small group of people in my part of the country who are non-stipendiary priests, we call them in the Anglican Church, or worker priests, which is my preferred title. One is a barrister, for example, and another is a systems analyst for a company that makes guided missiles: he sort of plays World War III on a computer. When I meet the lawyer, what I would like to hear is some reflection about the relationship between divine justice and what happens in his court. That's what I understand his area of expertise to be. But he doesn't tell me that. He tells me about how one of his colleagues has died and he counseled his wife. Now, I'd be the last person to say that was unimportant. That's really, really important. But it's of sort of general importance, I'd say, and what I want from this person is something particular about the world. I want to know how the world works and how God works in that world where he is. I don't hear that from Christians very much.

I met a priest who is a coroner. He presides over a court that hears about deaths of one sort or another. We had a very big fire in Britain in a football stadium. It was a horrible fire in which many people died. He was the coroner at the court that heard all this evidence. He spoke with extraordinary understanding about how these people wanted to know all the details about how their loved ones had died. He said that specific information, like what positions the bodies were in when they died, is really important to these people. You have to tell them how the body was positioned exactly and what clothing was left. It's a kind of liberation of their grief, he said. Introducing the survivors of the dead to the people who owned the football stadium is to effect a kind of reconciliation. He said, "I've seen the most profound acts of forgiveness in my court, cases where people have died most horrifically in industrial accidents, and their relatives have said across my court to the person who owns the factory, 'Look, I know it's not your fault that my husband fell into this machine,' or whatever." It is very moving to sit at the feet of someone like this and think, Gosh, this person really understands the world.

Yet, so often, when people with this kind of experience put their religious clothes on, what they have to say comes out sounding inept and embarrassing. What happens is that donning the priestly robes makes them lose their authority. That's what the Church seems to be asking me to do all the time. On that level, I would say that almost weekly I become more pessimistic, or rather I am brought back to this rather sobering feeling that my ministry is not going to effect much change here. I do see it as profoundly important for me to come into the college of priests. I'm not a believer in priests being the same as other people – in the sense that all ministries in the church are the same. There are specific characters about our ministries and I'd like to sit in my college of priests or with the Bishops and, after a reflective silence, I'd like us to say to one another, "Look, this is what the world is like where I am." I cannot find that. I find that profoundly depressing because it has something to do with the church's inability to take the world seriously. For a religion which is supposed to be incarnational, it is deeply troubling to find this simple lack of interest in what flesh is like. On this level I'm pessimistic. In other ways I'm fairly optimistic. Here there does exist quite an openness about understanding that the relationship between religion, science, art and culture is very complex. I think I am optimistic at the level of feeling that there is a degree of rapprochement between realms which have been separate, or seen as separate, for quite some time. Perhaps the European temperament is a little more comfortable with this.

SLACK: Well, I think it's more mature.

RODWELL: Maybe. It has its problems, but in some respects, maybe.

SLACK: Of course, as you said, there may be some benefits to America's adolescence, too.

RODWELL: Yes. Horizontality, for example. We did a training course for the US Nature Conservancy three years ago. When I was in Wisconsin, I met the chief ecologist of TNC and he came over here with ten of his staff and we went to the center of the Lake District, which is a sort of modestly mountainous part of north-western Britain, and you can see about fifty miles. We said, "Let's try and position ourselves and calibrate our view of the landscape. How many mapping units can you see?" And they just looked around briefly and said, "Well, one actually. It's sort of grass with trees." And I thought, "This is fantastic, that kind of pioneer view of looking outwards to the horizon." That's wonderful.

4 Brian Cantwell Smith

The Language of Matter

Brian Cantwell Smith is professor of cognitive science, computer science and philosophy, adjunct professor of the history and philosophy of science, and assistant director of the cognitive science program, at Indiana University in Bloomington, Indiana. Before moving to Indiana in 1996, he was principal scientist at the Xerox Palo Alto Research Center (PARC) and adjunct professor of philosophy at Stanford University. He was a founder of the Center for the Study of Language and Information (CSLI) at Stanford, a founder and first President of Computer Professionals for Social Responsibility (CPSR) and president of the Society for Philosophy and Psychology.

Smith's research focuses on the foundations and philosophy of computing and on the use of computational metaphors in other fields such as cognitive science, physics and art. He compares today's computer hackers to the pre-scientific alchemists of the fifteenth century, and suspects we are on the cusp of a scientific revolution at least as profound as the original one. Today's revolution, however, concerns the "intentional" sciences, a variety of practices ranging from the nuts and bolts of computer programming to the most abstract realms of philosophy, involving issues of symbols, representation and meaning. To understand how one thing – such as a word or thought or binary code or photon – can effectively represent another, we have to address fundamental mysteries about the mind's relationship to the world. Pursuing these mysteries may lead, he says, to an understanding of meaning that, if done properly, just might restore the other kind of meaning to a world in spiritual crisis.

BRIAN CANTWELL SMITH: I grew up as a member of the United Church of Canada. On top of that, my father was a theologian and professor of comparative religion (technically also an ordained minister, though he worked as an academic, not as a preacher). In profound ways, I've been influenced by his work. Though I've worked in and around the sciences, there's a sense in which you can see me as running the family store. There's tremendous continuity between the issues that come up in my work and his world view: his sense of significance, his sense of what it is to be religious, the basic theological perspectives he taught us as children.

My father's theology was radical in many ways. For example, he wrote books arguing against the idea that *propositional belief* is at the core of any religious tradition. Many people think that to be religious is to *believe* certain things: like, say, that God exists, or that some day we'll go to heaven. I suspect most people in this country think that to be Christian is to believe certain things, of that form. But my father argued against this idea that you can reduce "being religious" to assent to propositional claims. In fact he thought it was fatal: that the religious traditions would die, if they – mistakenly – insisted on propositional assent.

Did I grow up with a religious background? Absolutely. Does that mean I believe in God? Or that I believe this or that? The answer is probably "no," to questions of that form. I want to get underneath those formulations, not to assent to or deny them.

I thought a lot about these things as a kid. When I was twelve, I refused to be confirmed because I couldn't believe the things they were telling me at church. Later, when I got to college, I quit going to church entirely. And I haven't really had what anybody on the outside – or inside! – would call a religious practice, since. But I never stopped struggling with the underlying metaphysical and theological questions: What's the nature of being? What are the grounds of ethics? Those things have always mattered to me. Where to find grounding, how to anchor your life, how to know what's worth committing to.

GORDY SLACK: How, then, would you describe your religious practice?

SMITH: Well, in terms of what "practice" means to most people, the answer is probably "I don't have one."

SLACK: What about in your own terms? Can you distinguish between those activities you engage in that are religious and those that aren't?

SMITH: No, that distinction doesn't mean much to me, either. I don't use the word "religious" much at all. It's not that I feel one should wrestle with these things in private. In fact I think it's critical that the struggles not be private. The problem with the words "religion" and "religious," though, is that they are such triggers, both for people who like the words and for people who are allergic to them. In general, I don't usually find myself having any more in common with people who consider themselves religious than with people who don't. In fact on particular issues – especially of belief! – I often side with atheists and agnostics.

When I told my Dad I was quitting going to church, because I didn't believe the things on which they required assent, he said I was probably right to refuse. "The sad thing is," he said, "that you and your friends, if you opt out of religious community, are going to lose vocabulary in which to talk among yourselves about the things that matter to you most." So I asked him what he thought it was to be religious. His answer: "To find the world significant."

Thirty years on, I still believe him. A great many people in my post-Second-World-War generation have lost vocabulary that can mean, for them, what it is that religious vocabulary means to people who think of themselves as religious.

Given all that, do I have a religious practice? Well, there's no one facet of my life reserved for "religious stuff." It's not a distinct sub-species of life to me, not a practice in the sense that each morning I do X, each Friday I do Y, or anything like that. It undergirds the whole thing. Does it have to do with ultimate issues, with the world's significance? Absolutely. Does it affect how I live my life? – what walk I walk? Definitely. Something like, "What religious issues have meant to people who are religious, underneath the level of the explicit affirmations" – that's extremely important.

There are real problems of vocabulary. I find it very difficult to find words that come close to communicating to people I know the things that matter most. I often end up using different words with different people. Maybe that seems hypocritical or opportunistic. But I don't believe it. I do it in order to be more accurate, not less. Still, it's a struggle.

I'm pretty sure people who are "religious," in the sense I use the word, will find my book *On the Origin of Objects* a religious book. At the same time, I hope people who *aren't* religious *won't* find it religious. That's not because there's a hidden meaning for just "religious" folks to see. Rather, there's something important to me, something I am trying to get across in this book. People who don't think of themselves as religious may perfectly well "get it"; they just won't think of *that kind of thing* as religious. That's fine. I don't care how people categorize it. All in all, in fact, I'd rather duck the "r-word." What I care about is that we learn how to talk to each other about things that matter.

SLACK: Do you think that there are people who *don't* find the world significant? Can you be a human being and not find significance in the world?

SMITH: That's a crucial question. Before I answer, I should say that I don't presume "significance" is something that you either have or don't have, find or don't find, in a black-and-white way. I don't even think of it as something you have in a *continuous* way. "Black-and-white" and "continuous" are inadequate ideas to get at the thick meaning of a fully lived life.

Given all that: then yes, I do think there are people who don't find the world significant. But it's tragic. In not finding it significant, they fall short of expressing their full humanity.

What especially worries me are people who look and do not find. There's enormous dissatisfaction around that question these days – people who feel anonymous, that their lives are hollow or unsatisfying, that social and economic conditions don't give them a chance at a satisfying life – and so on. You know what I mean. It's almost a platitude to say this sort of thing – though just because it's a platitude doesn't mean it isn't true.

Think about the rise of religious fundamentalism: the Christian right in this country; ultra right-wing Zionists in Israel; fundamentalist Muslims in the Near East and North Africa. People may think of these as separate phenomena. The press certainly tends to treat them differently. But I think they're all very similar. There is a deep unsatisfied hunger in many people's lives, an unfulfilled yearning. People feel that materialist values, capitalist economic values and so on, just aren't satisfying. The ideals espoused on TV and in popular culture don't give them the kind of grounding, the kind of community, the sense of transcendence, the feeling of significance, that they would like. Fundamentalist movements recognize that gnawing lack, that hollowness and frustration and try to provide answers.

Problem is, I find the fundamentalists' answers appalling. In fact they scare me stiff. Wittingly or not, fundamentalist movements cater to closed-mindedness, bigotry and fascism. But what are we intellectuals, we academics, we scientists, providing by way of response to that yearning? If we don't have answers, we don't have a leg to stand on, to criticize the fundamentalists.

What we need are *better* answers – answers that do justice to people, in their plural ways of being; answers that avoid the bad aspects of fundamentalism; answers that inspire, in the literal sense of giving people breath and hope; answers that unify, rather than divide; answers that feed that palpable hunger for anchoring, meaning, significance. That's what I want to do for the next twenty-five years: I want to help work on formulating betters answer to those questions.

A footnote. One of the reasons some non-religious people are allergic to religion is because they worry about this way of putting things. The real problem, they say, is economic conditions and social injustice. Any effort to come up with a "religious" response to appalling conditions, to the absence of sustaining work, to street violence and homelessness and so forth, they view as at best window-dressing and at worst fascism. I support much of what they say: yes, we have to correct economic injustice; that's part of what I take to be a condition on a palatable answer. On the other hand, I don't think economic conditions are enough. Hollow lives aren't a prerogative of the underclass.

SLACK: Science is one place many people look when they've turned away from fundamentalist theologies, or moderate theologies for that matter. I wonder if the kind of anchoredness and significance you talk about can actually be found in science? On the other hand, many of the scientists I know best are "religious" in their zeal to *subtract* significance and value from their scientific perspective.

SMITH: I'll tell you a story. I have a friend who is a very serious Jew. He devotes a day or so a week to questions of Talmudic interpretation, religious ritual and so on. It's a significant part of his life. He is also a "big-S" scientist: he worked for a while at Bell Labs, is now chair of a computer science department. We were good friends in graduate school, and this sort of question – about the juxtaposition of the scientific and the religious – preoccupied us both. The funny thing – and it struck us both at the time – is that I was completely unprepared to do what he was entirely content with. He viewed his scientific work as religious, in a way that, to him, was perfectly satisfying. I just couldn't do the same thing. He was happy; I was torn apart.

I visited him several years later, and at one point burst out laughing. "I finally figured it out!" I said. "You want your scientific work to be *worship*. I want my scientific work to be *theology*."

To get to your question: One of the things people in science have historically tried to do, of course, is to subtract or "disappear" the issue of value. That's part of the "value-free" mythology of science. But note that we don't eliminate *truth*, which is a big value. If I come up with a theory that's false, that's no good, on anyone's account. Even traditionalists have to agree that at least one "norm" (as philosophers call them) is operating in science: the norm of truth.

Given that, consider the Greek separation of values into truth, beauty and goodness – three basic normative dimensions of life – and ask why science has hung on to truth and let go of beauty and goodness. It is not as trivial a question as it might look. It's something of a default *modus operandi* for science, these days, to valorize truth, ignore goodness, and perhaps allow a little beauty back in to dance over the elegance of the equations. Is that the best we can do?

I'm very respectful of the reason people want to keep values – other than truth – out of science. What I want to argue is that we can – increasingly *must* – let some other values back in – especially ethical ones. But – this is critical – I want to do so in a way that respects why science originally threw them out, and doesn't compromise, *one iota*, the truth to which science has been dedicated for so long.

Why did people throw values out? Think about why people defend "value-free" science – "truth, the whole truth, and nothing but the truth." They have perfectly legitimate fears of what might happen if we were to abandon that high standard. They're afraid that by doing so we would open ourselves up to prejudice, bigotry, suspicion, obfuscation, lying, despotism and a whole bunch of other reprehensible things. I agree that those things are terrible. I absolutely don't want to license more inquisitions, applaud rank subjectivity, or legitimate the crude, unchecked exercise of political power. It was genuinely liberating for science and rationality to free us, during the Scientific Revolution, from such forms of oppression.

Problem is, that "freeing" move is not enough. It's not enough to keep the bad things out of science. It's time to bring some good things in. When people were explicitly religious, as well as scientific, they could keep non-truth values out of science, and then lean on their religious traditions to show them what was good, what to do, how to live. I don't think we can afford to divide the norms that way any more: handing truth over to science, and goodness to disparate religions. We need reconciliation – we need to bring them back together again.

And we've got to do so effectively. No one who's involved in social action believes that just having a *theory* of politics is enough. Ultimately you also have to *do* something. If we are to fight for the things we believe in, and fight *against* the things we *don't* believe in (I mean "believe" in the etymologically original sense of "caring" or "giving your heart to"), then we have to be instructed jointly: in the ways of power, the ways of goodness, the ways of truth. It all has to be integrated. We have to fight, powerfully, for what is right and good and true.

That, of course, raises the question of what *is* right. "Right according to whom?" To get at that, think about what's happening in science. A while back, I used the word "significance." There's a story to be told about that word. Since its rise in the sixteenth and seventeenth century, you can think of natural science as having gone through a tremendous several-hundred-year ascendance. Recently, though, the edifice has started cracking. Since the war and the atomic bomb, people have begun to worry about the untrammeled "march of science" – wonder whether it won't do us in, whether it's really good for us and so on. Nobody would deny, though, that for hundred of years it has been a spectacular success.

Before the Scientific Revolution was the era of the alchemists. Once science arrived, they were shunned – remained unappreciated for hundreds of years. Once Newton and Maxwell were in place, that is, the alchemists looked as if they had been doing crazy stuff. But the story's not so simple. Recently, people have come to realize that the alchemists were not so crazy after all – and very important to the rise of science.

I believe the twentieth century will ultimately be recognized for the emergence of a transition on the same scale as the rise of natural science. I don't have a good word to express it, but it's basically an investigation into things having to do with meaning or interpretation or symbols or representation or information. Philosophers call it the realm of the "intentional"; the realm of the "semiotic" might be better, except that "semiotics" has such strong connotations, in some quarters, that many people are as allergic to it as other people are allergic to the word "religion." One way to describe this new science is as an emerging understanding of signs, signifying, signification – if you take those words broadly enough. The things that are the basis of anything semiotic or epistemic or intentional. Whatever we call it, it's basically a realm of *meaning*. You see it in mathematics; you see it in set theory. You see in the realm of the computer, symbol manipulator or information processor. You see it in psychology, in people's use of representations and information. You see it in linguistics, anthropology, economics, and increasingly in biology. Meaning is such a profound phenomenon that I take this wildfire spread of interest as indicative that we're on the cusp of a whole new scientific era.

For several hundred years, "natural" science meant "physical" science. What I think we're going to see – maybe for another few centuries – is a new kind of "natural" science, that fuses matter with meaning: something like semiotic or intentional science.

The original alchemists tried to turn iron into gold. I think we're in an analogous era of "pre-understanding." All those C++ and Java programmers are "semiotic alchemists," trying to turn code into gold! For fifty years we've had a widespread, inarticulate, dedicated, rather disheveled practice of people trying to construct arbitrary things out of mechanism, symbols, meaning, information. Just like the fourteenth century. And I wouldn't be too surprised, once we finally get our heads around this new stuff, if this first century of programmers were laughed at and shunned, were thought to be just messing around uselessly – the way, for so many years, we laughed at the alchemists. But I'd also bet that present-day programmers are in fact – and will ultimately be recognized to be – as important as the original alchemists in setting the stage for an intellectual revolution.

What does this have to do with religion? Here's the catch. Signs, signifying, signification, and— significance! But as we saw at the beginning, "significance" means importance! What is significant isn't just what has been mentioned or symbolized or represented or referred to, but what *matters*.

So now we get to the million-dollar question: If twentieth-century developments – computing, logic, psychology, mathematics, linguistics, anthropology, biology and so forth – are really bringing us to the verge of a new era in science, a new era that will take on not just the physical world, but also the world of symbols and meanings and signifying, what will this new era have to say about *real significance* – the kind that has to do with being religious? Is the "signifying" that science will study restricted to simple sorts, like the link from smoke to fire? Or is there a chance, when all is said and done, that we won't be able to take on those simple questions without unleashing larger questions of importance? In other words: is this new era of science going to require a broadening of our sights to include not just the factual, but also the ethical?

SLACK: Can you subtract the value of significance in your scientific study of signifying? I suppose the last hundred years of anthropology has faced that puzzle.

SMITH: That's right. Of course some people would say that this is all a pun – that it's only an etymological accident that (i) "significance," in English, means "importance," and (ii) that the same word is used, technically, to refer to the property of signs, whereby they signify things. But I don't believe it's a pun at all. From what I can tell, from studying intentional systems, the simple smoke-means-fire properties of signification, and the full ethical properties of what is important – how it is to "live truly" – can't ultimately be separated. Once science starts to encroach on one, it's inexorably going to find itself dealing with the other.

Signifying is also not the only notion with an ethical dimension. So is *materiality*. "Material evidence," in a court of law, isn't evidence that weighs some number of kilos, or that has an inertial mass, but evidence that makes a difference. Even the word "matter" has a normative dimension. Scientifically, we think of matter as "pure physical stuff." But to talk about what "matters" is also a way of describing what's important.

So one of the things I'm trying to do, in my writing, is to reclaim "materiality" for *the kind of thing that has importance*, and to pull it away from pure physicality. I defend this because I believe ordinary material objects are normatively constituted. To be an object is to be taken by an agent or society to be something that is *valued* as an object, something that one has to *defend* as an object, something that *matters*. When you say "A cup is a cup," you're staking a normative claim. A statement of object identity is a statement of values, not a statement of purely physical conditions.

In saying that objects matter, am I saying that objects are *more than material*? No, I'm saying that *materiality itself is normative*. So in a funny way I end up being more "materialist" than most people – certainly most religious people – would expect. But it's an incredibly expensive form of materialism.

SLACK: You want to re-imbue matter with mattering?

SMITH: Yes, re-imbue stuff with importance. *Put the mattering back into matter.* That's exactly right. And then, if we do that – this is the dream – maybe we can have an epistemic or intentional or semiotic "science" that actually understands "significance" in the ethical sense of importance. A science that does so in a *good*, not just *true*, way.

Now I should be careful. Dreams can crash and burn. I don't want to prejudge all this. I don't want to say I have an a priori commitment to a claim that importance does in fact derive from signification, in a way that this new scientific era is going to understand. Two or three hundred years from now, I can imagine – even if we have a kind of semiotic science or a broad range of sciences dealing with signification and interpretation and so on – that people of that day will say issues of mattering, emotion, social justice, et cetera, weren't done any more justice by the 300 years of intentional sciences than they were by the preceding 300 years of physical science.

But in spite of that caution, I believe there are very serious reasons to think we're going to make real progress in those realms. One of my most basic metaphysical commitments is that truth, beauty and goodness aren't completely separable. Just as physicists claim that gravity, charge, mass, et cetera, weren't separated, in the first 10^{-23} seconds of the universe, so too I don't think God made the world with truth, beauty and goodness fully separated, either. Oddly enough – this will seem sacrilegious to many people – you can see shadows of this in modern software design. Whether programs work well, whether they're beautiful, and whether they're right – these things aren't all that separable. In practice, it is impossible to maintain clean distinctions among these constitutive norms.

All I'm trying to do in this conversation is open up the possibility of these questions. Well, that's a lie! I'm trying to do more than that. I'm saying that ethics may not only have to be brought into our new subject matter; it may also have to be brought into our methods. Not just *true* theories of the-true-and-the-good. *True-and-good* theories of the-true-and-the-good.

SLACK: The philosopher Ludwig Wittgenstein said that when science has answered everything it can, the questions of life will remain untouched. You seem to be suggesting that the emerging science of semiotics, or whatever, may begin to say some things that do touch the "questions of life." On the other hand, I see you're remaining open-minded about that, you're not necessarily convinced that that's so, but you're opening up that possibility.

SMITH: That's right. I don't agree with Wittgenstein. I don't believe "Science can't touch what matters." Statements like that are rooted in a particular conception of science – one we've had for 300 years – which may not last. In fact I think statements like Wittgenstein's are intellectually irresponsible. They're just recipes for hiding one's head in the sand. If I'm right that a new framework is needed to understand this emerging "Age of Significance" then science will have to *change*, to incorporate values. And that will affect life. Stranger things have happened.

Religion may have to change, too – into something never before imagined. We need new theology as much as we need new science. We need a theology – brought up to date scientifically and altered to capture imaginations and inspire a world-wide community of diverse people – that can incorporate the full range of human questioning into ultimate significance, give people a reason to live and anchor their commitments, help people understand why they care about the people they care about and why they should care about things that are important. More profoundly – this is my special line – I believe the updated science and the updated theology will ultimately turn into the *same project*. I don't know exactly how this will go: what will fire the imagination, calm the spirit, do justice to the world, provide grounding for our lives. But I do know that it's absolutely urgent that we find out.

I try to take a tiny step in this direction in *On the Origin of Objects*, sketching a metaphysical conception of the world that, I think, just might be durable enough to underwrite both projects, or their fusion. The basic claim is that no other form of metaphysical foundation – and no foundation we've had in the past – is strong enough even to underwrite science and computing and other mundane things, let alone questions of importance and ultimate significance. As I said above, even such obvious questions as what kind of thing an individual entity is, can't be answered, I believe, except with respect to an ethical frame, which already starts to encroach on topics of traditional religious interest. Having to decide if a fetus is alive, in the case of abortion for example, is a question of individuals – and needless to say is a question that matters. If you're going to act, based on your answer, you'd better know what your commitments are. No scientist can answer whether there's a person there, without recognizing it as an ethical – even sacred – question. Not only does it have ethical consequences; it's ethically *based*. No non-ethical science can do justice to the notion of individuality.

SLACK: Is it possible that a computer scientist, in trying to develop a machine that could recognize individual objects, would provide the answer to the question of what constitutes an individual?

SMITH: It's unlikely that a computer scientist would stumble on the answer. What I'm saying is that, in order to build a machine to recognize individual objects, one has to locate it within a whole ethical framework in terms of which to make such judgments. Willy-nilly, programmers inscribe ethical assumptions in their code. If computer scientists write programs that make decisions based on judgments of individuality, and those systems are deployed in society, then those systems are ethically implicated. The question is, what responsibility do programmers bear in constructing systems that make that kind of decision?

These aren't entirely abstract questions. About fifteen years ago, a bunch of us were involved in starting an organization called Computer Professionals for Social Responsibility (CPSR). We were concerned about a lot of things, but what initially focused the organization were concerns about Ronald Reagan's Star Wars Initiative, and issues about launch and warning – issues, incidentally, that are coming back to haunt us, in proposals for an antiballistic missile shield. We worried that the Pershing II missiles in Eastern Europe were set on computer-based "launch on warning" status, since you have only about eight minutes after first detection to get your missiles out of the ground, otherwise they'll be destroyed. Our question: can you trust a computer system to make the right decision – i.e., decide the fate of Europe – in eight minutes? Our answer: *no*. Neither a person, nor a machine, should ever do that. The fate of Europe is simply not the sort of thing that should be decided in eight minutes. It's not the kind of judgment that can be properly made in that amount of time.

At the time, we encountered left-wing fundamentalists who said, "You should never trust a computer with human life." But I don't believe that. I land at the San Francisco Airport in the fog all the time. I'm glad there aren't pilots peering out the windows trying to find the runway. In fact I think that being landed automatically by radar, or at least being substantially assisted by radar, is quite possibly far and away the best thing to do in such situations. But if that's true, then you have to face up to the question: "What can you trust computer systems with?" Very quickly, that brings you up against questions of what it is to trust, what kinds of decisions there are, how we understand issues of that sort and so on. Making a taxonomy of the ethical structure of the decisions computers are implicated in is terrifically difficult. The thing is, though – and this is the point – it's something that we are tacitly doing all the time. We're doing it because computers are already deployed throughout society, often in so-called "mission-critical" applications.

Although a mathematician originally invented them, computers aren't theoretical objects any more. They are participants in the world, along with us. They have material properties. They have economic properties. They have ethical properties. They affect political decisions. So our responsibility, as computer scientists and philosophers and social theorists, is to come up with an understanding of computers that meets the challenge they pose.

SLACK: Technological progress depends a lot on looking at things in new ways, in honoring innovation, and in trying on different pairs of glasses, so to speak, until you've seen things in a light that enables you to do new things. A lot of religion emphasizes the importance of seeing things in a traditional way, of reminding oneself how things are to be understood, or why certain things are good and other things bad. How do you move back and forth between this striving for new interpretations and at the same time honor the past and the significance that we obviously inherit from it?

SMITH: Institutionally, there's truth to what you say. Certainly the myth of scientific research is a constant emphasis on "new, new, new." And admittedly, too, most religious myths don't have this "ever new" emphasis. But some of them nevertheless emphasize searching – though of a more personal form. Many years ago I was married to a Quaker and for a while attended Quaker meetings. You know George Fox's notion – that there is "that of God in every person," with the concomitant rejection of the priesthood and so on – that each person's salvation is for him or her to find. In this sense the notion of searching is as religious as it is scientific.

On the other hand, you are surely right that exploring the new is not as heavily institutionalized on the religious side as in science. So much the worse for theology! Surely it must change, too, to come to understand the world better, as urgently as science.

It would be tragic, in fact, if religious traditions didn't figure out new things. Think of the urgent problems they face. How can they simultaneously have faith in their own traditions, yet recognize the validity of other religious traditions? Can they help the rest of society develop a way to incorporate the generosity and justice of pluralism without compromising excellence, standards and value? How can we have a pluralist world view that is neither vacuous nor shallow? Presumably it's too late in history for any religious leader any longer to say or believe anything of the form: "We're right; you're wrong." Yet, at the same time, it would be terrible if religious leaders were to water down their conviction to something like, "It doesn't matter what you believe; we all have our stories." Both of these positions – these limit cases – are profoundly untenable. But what is a viable middle ground? Or is it even a question of "middle"?

Formulating it this way shows how intertwined the religious issues are with intellectual and scientific ones. There is no more important question for society at large, I believe, than how to combine appropriate respect for pluralism with deep recognition of value.

SLACK: Let me change direction for a second and talk about God. In your book you write, "The world has no other." Unless the world itself is defined as God – a definition that might wear out pretty quickly for its simplicity – is there any room in this perspective for God?

SMITH: Was it Tillich who said God was the "ground of being"? To the extent I understand the word "God" at all, it *is* as a word for everything. For me, the term "God," or anyway the only sense of it that I find meaningful, is as a reminder connoting the "moreness," yet ultimate unity, of everything. I think it's part of the muezzin's cry to say, "I know that Allah is greater than I know him to be." There's a wonderful humility implicit in that phrase. And yet, at the same time, it's traditional to believe that there is "no thing that is more than God."

"God" absolutely does not mean anything to me like a person or anthropomorphized figure – an old man with grey hair. It doesn't mean anything that has a distinctive agency in the world different from physical causation, or that is in any other way *separate* from the world we inhabit. There are Kabbalistic stories, I understand, about how at the beginning of the universe God had to evacuate a space within himself in order to make room for the world to exist. That's wonderful poetry and it makes a splendid point, but I confess I don't believe it. I suspect my notions are much more Buddhist than anything recognizably Judeo-Christian.

So to get to your question, I don't, ultimately, think that "the world" and "God" are different. They both refer to everything there is. "The world" is a cheap way to refer to it;

"God" is an expensive way. What's critical, though, is to understand that equation (that "God" and "the world" both refer to "all that there is") not as cheapening God, but as increasing the worth of the world. This is something mystics understand: that the complete and total world – "everything there is" – vastly, awesomely, unutterably transcends what most people *think* the world is.

Put it this way: you only need God to transcend the world if you have an impoverished world. There's enormous truth to that claim that "we see through a glass, darkly."

SLACK: In *On the Origin of Objects* you write that "there is nothing larger than the world."

SMITH: Yes, again this is an issue of communication. If you are talking to someone who has a modest, garden-variety, mundane sense of the world – just physical objects, things like that – then it's useful to have a word, like "God," that refers to radically more – to "the whole totality." It's tricky, of course; names usually require a figure/ground separation, but "the totality" can't be a figure, because there's no ground to define it against. For a shorthand way of orienting towards everything, in its stupefying totality, maybe "God" is a good word. My worry is that reserving a special term like "God," rather than "world," to name everything sets you up to radically underestimate the world. Remember where we started: to be religious is to find the *world* significant.

But in the end I don't care about particular words. What matters to me is to find terms that we can all – including people who are allergic to religious vocabulary – use to mean ultimate things. How are we going to speak to our friends about what matters most?

For most civilizations, over most of their histories, the religious traditions were where such ultimate questions got framed. If we can't frame them, we aren't going to find answers. If we are going to talk to each other, we need language to refer to that from which importance is derived.

SLACK: And where significance is derived, too.

SMITH: Yes – but again it's tricky. For example, you can ask whether people derived their sense of significance from their religious traditions, or whether the traditions were institutions that allowed people to talk about where they derived their sense of significance from. More the latter, I suspect. That is, it seems more historically accurate to say *not* that you derive your significance from church or from going to church, but that going to church reminds you of your significance.

SLACK: They might say you derived your significance from God.

SMITH: That's right. So I ask: "What is God, such that you derive your significance from Him?" And on that, people vary. Some people think of God as a delineated individual: "personal," but different from themselves. As I've indicated, that's not something I understand.

This goes back to your earlier suggestion that science searches for new ways of understanding, whereas the religious traditions largely don't. It seems urgent for the religious traditions to recognize that the term "God" isn't working as well as it used to – not only for people outside of religious communities, but for many within. This is especially true for conceptions of "God" as somehow *separated* from the world. In fact I'd argue that the idea of a "separated" God no longer makes any sense at all, in the context of enmeshed, modern science. In fact it seems like an outright dangerous idea. To license it – without some fancy concomitant explanation – is liable to engender a sense that religious understanding can part company with scientific understanding. Endorsing a "separate God" ducks responsibility for showing how the world is one. That seems shabby – scientifically, intellectually, theologically. Showing how the world is one is exactly the sort of ultimate question religious traditions should focus on.

SLACK: If to be religious is "to find the world significant," God might be defined as that which makes the world significant. But there may not be that much you can say beyond that.

SMITH: It seems to me that most religious traditions, when you push, don't say that "something makes things significant," but rather that things are significant in virtue of their existence – perhaps their divine existence. Significant in and of themselves, at the deepest level. If that's not Christian, then I guess I'm not a Christian; it's not for me to say what that tradition is. Though I admit that I think – for technical reasons, in part – that any attempt to formulate what the word "God" means, that tries to specify it in articulated terms, public language, is bound to fail. What's important, if we choose to keep that three-letter word around, is surely not something *articulated*.

If people could have a sense of what it is to live life so as to take the world seriously and find significance for themselves therein, then I think a practice might grow up in which people used the three-letter word to remind each other of that common orientation. Maybe it would; maybe it wouldn't. I don't really care, though I'm not particularly enamored of the word "God." But ultimately what matters is the orientation, not the formulation.

In closing, I should say I have enormous respect for how hard it is to say *any* of these things in tenable ways. Poetry is some help. A poem can orient you towards things that it itself need not name. People also understand that, even if poems aren't factual, that they're not thereby false. Similar things, I think, go on in religious language. Unfortunately, poetry is too marginalized in society, these days – at least here in the US – to play as important a role as we need. Given the current scientific, technological, economic and political state of the industrial West, I don't think poetic language alone will allow people to forge a strong enough collective sense of purpose, or adequately give voice to the things that matter to us, individually and collectively.

So what language will work? I don't know. It's an urgent question, without obvious answer. One thing I do know: we mustn't presume that we know how language works, and then, based on that presumptive understanding, try to forge a language that will articulate our sense of significance. Current theories of language are too rooted in the prior scientific, formalist era. Fortunately, though, language itself isn't hobbled by what we currently and mistakenly *think* language is. Language is fertile, fecund – and nowhere near exhausted. So I'm still optimistic. Maybe we can find – even hammer out together – some language that will go the distance.

5 Bruno Guiderdoni
Reading God's Signs

Bruno Guiderdoni is an astronomer at the Paris Institute of Astrophysics. His research focuses on the formation and evolution of galaxies, a subject on which he has published more than eighty papers and organized several international conferences. From 1993 to 1999 he produced "Knowing Islam," a French public television program. He has also published widely on Islamic theology and mysticism.

With the Copernican revolution, humans lost their place at the center of the physical universe. But, says Guiderdoni, modern physics and astronomy have restored that privileged position in an enlightened form. Discovery of the Big Bang and insights about the curvature of space-time and the finiteness of the speed of light, Guiderdoni says, have put us back at the "center" of the observable universe, which extends back, equally far in all directions, toward the moment of the Big Bang. Furthermore, he says, the finely tuned conditions necessary for a stable universe, for the formation of galaxies and planets and for the evolution of the increasingly complex life forms on Earth – culminating with the human mind – are ample evidence of God's special intentions for human beings.

"Science is an endless story," Guiderdoni says, "but we human beings are limited in time and we want some definitive answers to our questions." Guiderdoni's readings and travel led him to Islam, which represented to him a middle point between his Western upbringing and the mystical Eastern religions that interested him as a young man. Westerners often prejudge Islam's posture toward science, mistaking the dogmatic, anti-science, fundamentalist branches of Islam for the entire tree. For his part, Guiderdoni finds plenty of room in the tradition for rigorous uninhibited research. Indeed, he says, an honest and persistent quest for knowledge is the foundation of Islam. Because he believes that the root of sin is ignorance, he quotes the advice of the Prophet Mohammed: "Look for knowledge from birth to death."

BRUNO GUIDERDONI: I became a Muslim ten years ago after a long spiritual path, my own readings and reflections on the nature of knowledge and the significance of human life, and a stay of two years in Morocco. I give lectures on Islam in France, Italy and other places in Europe. I am also in charge of a program on the French Channel, France 2, which is one of the State TV channels. Every Sunday morning, there are several religious programs, from Buddhism to Judaism and various Christian Churches. There is also an Islamic program, and I am in charge of doing what you are doing with me now, on the TV. I do interviews and I try to explore various questions in Islamic culture and religion.

PHILIP CLAYTON: What were your earlier religious influences, and how did you finally come to make a commitment to Islam?

GUIDERDONI: My father and mother are Christians but I was not raised in a religion. As I studied science, I found that something was missing in the scientific approach of the world. As I looked for other kinds of knowledge I became aware that my quest was a religious one. I don't know how it is in the US, but in France, modern education completely evacuates the notion of God. As a consequence, the young people do not have the words to explain what they are feeling. After reading and traveling, I finally became aware that my quest was a religious quest. I was very attracted by Eastern religions, especially by their emphasis on the pursuit of knowledge. Becoming a Buddhist, or a Taoist, or a Hindu was too big a step away. Becoming a Muslim is something between East and West. Islam presents itself as a religion in the middle between Western religions – Judaism and Christianity – and Eastern religions. I feel that I am always in the same current, which has been opened by Judaism and Christianity, but I also have the possibility of a window opened on Eastern religions. I found my way in Islam, even though, as you know, Islam is now affected by many problems, especially by violent fundamentalism. Of course, there are also many treasures in Islam and many possibilities for a spiritual life.

CLAYTON: So the attractiveness of Islam was that it incorporated parts of Judaism and Christianity, and yet stood somewhat closer to the Eastern traditions.

GUIDERDONI: That's right. Especially Islamic mysticism, which is called Sufism. It puts an emphasis on the realization of knowledge in a compassionate way, within the framework of monotheism, with theological concepts which are very familiar to us. The visions of man, of the world and of Creation, are very similar in Islam and in Judaism and Christianity. Ultimately, the aim of a religious life is knowledge. This is very important; my scientific quest and my religious quest both share the same quest for knowledge.

CLAYTON: Would you talk a little bit about what you were not getting from the pursuit of scientific knowledge alone?

GUIDERDONI: In the nineteenth century, science hoped to answer all questions. Modern science is very successful at addressing the question of how things occur. But it doesn't begin to satisfy the question of "Why things are as they are?" That nineteenth-century hope was not really science; it was ideology. Now, science focuses more on its main aim, the exploration of the world; it has less to say at the level of philosophy. In the past century, all the attempts to define the nature of scientific truth have failed. In science we have a very efficient method for increasing our knowledge of the world. But we are unable to say if a theory is true, if it is probably true, if it is wrong, or if it is probably wrong. Karl Popper's work was very important from this point of view.

The answers to our scientific questions give rise to other questions. Science is an endless story, which is very exciting. Unfortunately, we human beings are limited in time, and we want some definitive answers to our questions. The quest for this kind of answer is natural, even if it's not scientific but religious. This is the reason why I wasn't completely satisfied by my scientific practice.

CLAYTON: Was there anything in the limitations on knowledge that scientists themselves have emphasized in the past hundred years that contributed to your clear understanding of the need for a second way? For instance, the uncertainty at the quantum level with Heisenberg's work.

GUIDERDONI: On my intellectual path there were two important steps, two important readings. The first one was the philosophy of science, and particularly Popper's work, which I read when I was twenty. The other important step was the debate about the nature and the completeness of quantum mechanics. In France there was a lot of debate ten or twenty years ago. Bernard d'Espagnat gave lectures at the university where I was studying fifteen years ago. I was impressed by his brightness and intelligence, and especially by his analysis of the limits of quantum mechanics and by the idea that reality is never fully accessible to scientific investigation. Reality is "veiled." I felt I needed to explore other ways of getting knowledge about reality.

CLAYTON: Since your conversion to Islam, how do you view science and religious traditions as being relevant to each other? Do you see them as complementary, as integrated, or as very different spheres?

GUIDERDONI: I think they are complementary. As I told you, Islam strongly emphasizes the importance of knowledge in life in general and in religious life in particular. The root of sin is ignorance, or obscurity. "Look for knowledge from the birth to the death," said the Prophet. *Zhulm* is the Arabic term for sin and obscurity. It is possible to get out of this sin by the light of knowledge. So it is necessary to look for knowledge, all kinds of knowledge: the knowledge of this world and the knowledge of the hereafter.

One might consider scientific knowledge to be the knowledge of this world, and the knowledge of the hereafter could be some kind of religious knowledge. As a matter of fact, the difference is not so clear. In Islamic tradition, the knowledge that must be looked for is knowledge that is useful for mankind in general. The pursuit of knowledge cannot be separated from ethical values. Like everything in the world, science has an aim, which is God Himself. We cannot conceive the pursuit of knowledge independently from the pursuit of some kind of personal improvement.

CLAYTON: So your work as a scientist is not fully separate from your obedience as a Muslim. Is this what you are saying?

GUIDERDONI: Yes. There is no crisis between science and religion. There was nothing like Galileo's case in Islam. Islam is open to all kinds of knowledge. So, as a Muslim, I feel very comfortable in my scientific activity because I can interpret my research work as the pursuit of knowledge for this world, as the exploration of the richness and beauty of God's Creation.

CLAYTON: It almost sounds as if, in Islam, there is a need, or a requirement, to integrate your work as a scientist with your practice of Islam.

GUIDERDONI: Yes. As a Muslim, the trend for me is to integrate all my activities in a single path, in a single way of living and thinking. As God is one, man also has to be one. Any separation between the professional activity and the religious quest is not good.

We don't have to separate our scientific activity and our religious activity. It's just not true that knowledge and faith have nothing to say to each other, that they are completely different ways of approaching reality. This view is one of the defects of some approaches to religion in Western civilization, especially after Kant.

However, I also have to emphasize that scientific knowledge is not like religious knowledge. At each moment, we have to be aware of the nature of what we are doing; we are not praying in the same way as we are doing science. It is necessary to unify our activity, but we also need discrimination. We have to be very precise on this point.

CLAYTON: So the Kantian separation between the world of nature and the world of moral responsibility and freedom, which has influenced much Christian and Jewish thought in the last two or three centuries, would not be acceptable in Islam?

GUIDERDONI: No, because every human act has an ethical meaning. Religion pervades everyday life. There are explicitly ritual moments in the day; the five daily canonical Islamic prayers, for instance. But after that, all the moments of life are opportunities for ritual acts simply because they are an exploration of the world. And any exploration of the world promotes knowledge. Since it's a way of learning about God's Creation, it's also a way of worshipping.

CLAYTON: For Islam, as for Judaism and Christianity, the universe has not only an arrow of time, but also a designed telos, a God-given purpose. How does this notion of purpose sit with contemporary physics and astrophysics?

GUIDERDONI: In the Qur'an there are many verses that emphasize God's design in Creation. This design extends to the details of everyday life. Nothing has been done by chance. Everything is designed with a purpose. Everything is God's sign: *ayah*. This is an important word in Islamic tradition; it means that everything in the world, everything that appears to us, actually brings a teaching from God. So, here again it is very easy to read modern science within this paradigm of finality. I am fascinated by the contrast between the success of reductionism, as a tool, as a methodological program, and its failure as a philosophical program. Our exploration of the details of the physics of the cosmos now leads to something that is easily readable as finality. All these "coincidences" which are "interpreted" by the anthropic principle, can be easily read as finality in the world. As a Muslim, of course, there is no effort to read that. The problem is rather for non-believers who have to conceive of the world as a huge building that lies on a very small number of finely tuned pillars, the values of the constants of physics. It's a problem for them.

CLAYTON: What is the argument, speaking as a physicist, for design and purpose in a created universe?

GUIDERDONI: Much work has been done on the anthropic principle, which is well summarized in John Barrow's book, *The Anthropic Cosmological Principle*. Historically, the vastness of the cosmos has been used as an argument against religion; the argument goes that if the cosmos is so extended, man is nothing and the concept of a revealed religion on the small planet where we are living has no sense. But we now know that the age of the universe and the size of the observable universe are intimately linked to our presence on earth. We could not have appeared in a cosmos with a different age and size. The old age of the universe is necessary for heavy element enrichment, which is necessary for the formation of planets and the appearance of life. The size of the universe is a consequence of its age, and so we need this space around us and this time behind us in order to be here now on earth.

CLAYTON: Some people have given physical arguments to defend the so-called strong anthropic principle. Are you sympathetic to the view that it was necessary that intelligent life would arise and that this necessity was built into the universe from the very beginning?

GUIDERDONI: Yes, I am. I think that it's an unavoidable consequence of recent works in modern cosmology. All of these "coincidences" on the physical constants make the very great complexity possible. As a believer, I hold the strong version of the anthropic principle: everything has been designed in such a way as to make the appearance of man possible.

CLAYTON: May I ask you about the nature of that principle? Some people would say that it is a metaphysical explanation. Others would say it's actually a physical conclusion, that this is something that we can derive from physics without stepping into metaphysics.

GUIDERDONI: For the moment, I would say that this is not a physical principle. It is something that has roots in science, but it is a metaphysical principle. This is a surprising return to metaphysics because many philosophers would have stated that we killed metaphysics as Kantian philosophy developed at the end of the eighteenth century. Now metaphysics has reappeared where it was least expected, from science itself.

I don't think the anthropic principle can be considered a physical principle, because a physical principle has to be predictive. I don't know whether any predictions have come from the anthropic principle. But surely we cannot evacuate it just because it has a metaphysical meaning.

CLAYTON: In the science of the last decade, as you describe it, metaphysical conclusions are implied by the work in astrophysics, and perhaps even are testable in some way. Physical research could actually provide evidence for one metaphysical view or another. Am I correctly describing your position?

GUIDERDONI: Yes, you are. The trend in Islam is always toward unity. So, saying that metaphysics can be completely evacuated from any field of human activity or knowledge is completely inconsistent with Islamic thought. From the point of view of modern science, which, at least in the last century, attempted to exclude metaphysics, the comeback is a surprise. Islamic thought emphasizes the intimate link between the description of the cosmos and its roots in metaphysical and spiritual principles. The success of reductionism, as a scientific methodology, and its failure as a philosophical program, are strong encouragement for the pursuit of scientific knowledge, and also for the pursuit of another kind of knowledge, another kind of seeing the unique truth. I think that all Islamic thought also converges to say that there is only one kind of truth. We have several ways of getting to this truth. Science is one way. Both its success and its failure are encouraging. The failure, that is, the absence of radical answers, is, perhaps, an incentive to go to other ways of getting truth. Perhaps a religious way is privileged, in some sense. I don't think that modern philosophy strongly emphasizes the research of truth. It was evacuated with the loss of metaphysics. So, perhaps religion is the only path that is left to scientists to try to get truth.

CLAYTON: So it might be something like this: that as a scientist, I am amazed by the improbability that I, as knower, should be here in the first place. When I look at the universe, it seems as if it were fine-tuned so that life could arise. I hear talk of an anthropic principle in physics, or of the importance of the observer in quantum physics, and I think there must be some purpose for us. I turn to religion to tell me, more fully, what that purpose is and what my own moral responsibility is before God. Is this the idea?

GUIDERDONI: That's exactly the point. I don't like dualistic interpretations of science, and particularly of quantum mechanics. I like reality; I am a realist. We think that there is a hidden reality, a "veiled reality," as d'Espagnat would say. We are trying to get closer to this reality with science, and we succeed in some sense. But we feel that we need a qualitative step, and this qualitative step addresses the question of the meaning of things. We can have an answer only through the religious approach, I think. And this is the reason why I see the two activities as completely complementary.

CLAYTON: Islam, like the other Western religions, teaches that human beings are created as morally responsible, as free, and as capable of relationship with God. How does this notion of person, the human being as person, fit with contemporary theory in the sciences?

GUIDERDONI: It is a related question; man is described in the Qur'an as God's vice regent on earth. So he is not at the top of Creation. One would say, perhaps, in Western civilization, especially in the Cartesian view of the world, that only man has a soul; so he can act in the world however he wants. In Islam, man is not at the top of Creation, but at the center of Creation. And we have to rule this Creation, in the name of God, as good gardeners. We are responsible for the Creation, and we cannot change the Creation as we want. Man appeared on earth as the consequence of an incredible number of crises in the evolution of the universe: crises in galaxy formation, stellar formation, star evolution and so on, up to the formation of planets and the appearance of life, and all the periods of life development and so on. Science is teaching us that we are on the top of a huge cosmic building, which lasted for ten billion years. Islam helps me feel comfortable because of its emphasis on knowledge and ethical values. Knowledge cannot be pursued independently from the quest of ethical values. The original ethical value was responsibility. So this scientific view, according to which man is the result of an incredible number of so-called "coincidences" and crises, should lead to a religious view in which man has a strong responsibility on earth.

Moreover, a very interesting thing is appearing in cosmology. The cosmological principle states that "far away" is like "here"; there is no privileged position in the cosmos. But this brings, also, the possibility of exploring the history of the universe. Because of the fact that far away is like here, the history of the universe can be addressed by looking at objects at high redshifts. This also means that far away gives an image of our remote past, because light travels at a finite speed. We can reconstruct the past of the universe, and our own past, up to the first moments after the Big Bang. So we have this central position; we are at the center of the observable universe. In some respects, our cosmos is very similar to the medieval cosmos, where man was also at the center of the world. Of course, we know that the world is infinite. But the observable world is a bubble around us. We have this kind of central position in building our knowledge of the world.

In another sense, we are in a good location to look at the universe because the plane of our Galaxy, for instance, has a good angle relative to the plane of the Local Super Cluster. We are not located in a molecular cloud and so on. The immediate universe around us, the Milky Way, is rather transparent. And we can have access to the remote past. If we lived in a starburst galaxy, or a molecular cloud, the universe would have been completely opaque around us, except for infrared and radio radiation. It would have been much more difficult to discover the universe.

There are similarities in our way of seeing the world and the medieval way of seeing the world. For medieval thinkers, the limit of the cosmos was the stellar sphere (or the Crystalline Sphere, more precisely, because of the discovery of the precession of the equinoxes). This was a sharp limit, the separation between the cosmos on one side, and the Empyreum [the locus of God's Throne] on the other side. This was the very limit for Creation. And we also have this kind of limit, because the limit of our observable universe is also a sphere. On its surface, we are at T=0 and we cannot see further; further is too remote a past. It's the moment of the Big Bang; it's the great mystery of modern cosmology. So we also have a kind of boundary between the world, the cosmos, which is describable by natural laws, and the mystery of the origin. The observable cosmos is a mixture of space and time which is characteristic of modern cosmology. We know that the world is infinite and full of stars and galaxies, but we have a dynamic view of the cosmos, an intimate link between looking at large distances and probing into the past. When we look far away, we are trying to probe our origins, exactly as Dante allegorically crossed the celestial spheres to see God's face. There are many similarities between the medieval cosmos and our modern view of the cosmos.

CLAYTON: I'm wondering how our knowledge of the evolution of life affects our religious view of the person. Evolutionary biology seems to tell us that we are very much like the other higher primates. Most of our genetic matter is shared in common. Does that present any tension for the religious belief in the uniqueness of the person as God's vice regent?

GUIDERDONI: There could be tension if you had a literal reading of the Holy Qur'an. But not if we have an open reading of the texts. Man's creation is described by the Qur'an: man is made by God with two elements. He is made from clay (*tin*) and from God's spirit (*Ruh*). This has been interpreted as an instantaneous creation. But there is nothing in the Holy texts that must unavoidably lead to this conclusion, because all that is described by evolution could be our clay part: the fact that we belong to the world, that we are a part of the cosmic evolution from the beginning, from the nucleosynthesis in stars and so on, and the fact that our elements, our "clay," was in the stars five billion years ago. This clay part makes us very close to the world, very close to the animals.

We also have another part, which is God's spirit. This spirit is a gift given by God, and it is not only reason. Aristotle would say that man is a reasonable animal, but reason isn't the only distinction. Unlike animals, humans have the capacity to know God, to realize His attributes and His qualities. In the Islamic tradition man is the only creature in the world that has the ability to realize all of God's Names, all of His attributes. This is the gift of God's spirit in us. There is nothing in Islam that contradicts the possibility that man's shape and man's qualities as an animal could have been acquired through a long period of evolution.

The Qur'an does not tell the history of the world. It is a different kind of book, a book which draws the attention of man to significant facts. It's not a scientific textbook. Parts of the Qur'an are very poetic and mysterious, and they can be read in different ways. During the Middle Ages, they were read literally, very similar to what has been done in Judaism or Christianity. But they are always open to interpretation and rereading.

The Qur'an states that there was a time during which man was not. Man is created for God, but the cosmos is created for man, to be the locus of our knowledge of God. The creation of man may have taken a very long time, but the amount of time is not really significant from a spiritual point of view. What matters is what is occurring now, our ability to understand God's acts in the cosmos.

CLAYTON: So the stories of how all of this came about and of how persons are different from other animals is less important in Islam than perhaps it would be in Christianity? The crucial question is the understanding of man today, before God, and how he lives and how he acts. Do I understand correctly?

GUIDERDONI: I think so. There is an emphasis in Islam on spiritual realization. This realization has a similar importance in Buddhism and Hinduism. We are used, as Western men, to trying to address many problems, and some of them may not be relevant for us. In spite of our great successes in the exploration of the cosmos, the aim of our creation is not the discovery of the cosmos. We have a very successful description of the history of the cosmos. But in spite of these discoveries, the important thing is missing: man's spiritual realization. For that, we need more knowledge than science can give us. We in the West are used to thinking that we can only know what we can transform into concepts. The Eastern religions, Islam also, which is Eastern from this point of view, teach that we can know much more than we can conceptualize. Of course, we are good at using our reason, at using our intelligence for its algorithmic power. But we also have another kind of intelligence. We have what medieval philosophers called "the intellect," the possibility of contemplating the truth. So if we want to address the question of origins, we have different kinds of answers. We have the answer given by modern cosmology and we also have the spiritual and mystical approach.

The complete answer can only be found in the Hereafter, which is also, according to Islamic tradition, the world of knowledge. On Earth, we are limited by the conditions of our world and we can only gain partial answers to the important questions. In the next world direct knowledge will be more accessible.

CLAYTON: And also the immediate intuition of *intellectus* would be available, whereas here, we have only limited ways of knowing, of modern reason, with its analysis, rather than synthesis.

GUIDERDONI: That's exactly the point. Here, we are very successful at algorithms. But we are forgetting that there is another path, that our intelligence is not only analytic, but also has a synthetic side, as you correctly said. This is also related to the mystery of scientific creativity, of scientific discovery. How can an idea appear in a scientist's mind? It's a big question. We can teach our students many things about science, but we are unable to teach them how to discover, because we have completely forgotten this contemplative side of the human mind and of human activity in general. In religion, we rediscover the importance of the contemplative path.

CLAYTON: Could it be that religious practice and observance could allow us to be more creative, could add to the analytic side a more holistic way of thinking?

GUIDERDONI: I think that's a possibility. We have the examples of holy men who were very creative, not only in Islam, of course, but in all religions. We have the impression that some kind of practice can open the mind, or help the mind get rid of barriers that are due to passions, to confusion and so on. And maybe this kind of practice can lead one to be more creative and more efficient in the world. But here again, that's not the main purpose of religious practice. The main purpose is not the discovery of the world; it's the action within the world in God's name, and through it, the discovery of God.

CLAYTON: It has been basic to Islamic belief that God not only is Creator, but also is the providential ruler, and in some sense, the controller of the universe. Has this understanding of God in the Islamic tradition grown through modern science, or remained unaffected by it, or has there been a challenge to the belief and the activity of God through our growing knowledge of the physical world?

GUIDERDONI: That is a very rich question and there are several answers, which differ according to the period of history we focus on. There is not much debate now between science and Islamic theology because Islamic theology has almost disappeared. We are in a difficult period in the Islamic world at the moment. There are two main trends in Islamic thought now: one can be called the rationalistic trend, or modernism, which accepts the results of modern science without criticism. This is a global acceptance of all the results of modern thought and technology, without any attempt to see whether they are consistent with Islamic thought or Islamic theology. The other is the fundamentalist point of view, according to which everything that comes from Western civilization is considered bad simply because it is Western. The fundamentalists want to elaborate an Islamic science, which would be parallel to modern science. The fundamentalists consider modern science Western science or Christian science. This is completely contrary to the great intellectual and spiritual tradition of Islam. So, unfortunately the debate in the modern Islamic world is very poor. There should be a third path between these two extreme ways of seeing the things.

Unfortunately, most Muslim thinkers are more interested in social matters than in fundamental matters because Islamic countries face so many economic and social problems. So most of the reflection in Islam is focusing on these problems. But historically, and for good reason, the trend of Islamic theology was to address fundamental matters first. We cannot properly address social problems, or economic problems, without a reflection on fundamental matters first. This is a great weakness in modern Islamic thought and it is the reason why modern Islamic reflection on social and economic problems is very frequently inadequate and why it can lead to the violence that we see today. At the root, the Islamic philosophy had disappeared by the end of the Middle Ages. Islamic thought has degenerated, except in the field of Sufism, where reflection has always been present but rather hidden. It's not easy to find a good book or a good person who has reflected on the question you asked.

CLAYTON: Do you understand your own work, for instance your work with French television, as part of an effort to help move Islamic theology to think about this question?

GUIDERDONI: I think that here, in Europe, we are better prepared to address these kinds of questions because we have the intellectual foundations. We have always lived with these questions. Maybe we are more prepared to think in a quiet way because we don't have to face the acute economic and political problems so many Muslim countries are facing. So we have the opportunity to have debates. For instance, I frequently go into mosques to give lectures on these problems and I see many young Muslims who have grown up here in Europe and received Western teachings and Western culture. They are waiting for this kind of reflection because it is necessary.

CLAYTON: So if we begin with the caveat that Islamic thinking in this area is at an early stage, and that the answer must be very speculative from a Muslim perspective, what is your own thinking about the relation of God, and God's activity in the world, and the physical description of reality.

GUIDERDONI: The Qur'an is not too clear on this. But there are two verses that seem very pertinent to me. One verse states that God created the world with mathematics. The Qur'an says that "the sun and the moon are ruled according to a computation." There are "numbers" in the cosmos. The Qur'an draws the attention of the reader to all the order that appears in the cosmos. There is also another verse, which states that "there is no change in God's Creation." That means that there are regularities; the order we see is there because there are regularities which were present from the beginning, and which can be identified, of course, with natural laws, which are created by God. God gives the possibility of natural laws. God is the condition of natural law.

CLAYTON: This would be an understanding of the action of God, which would be told in terms of the regularity of nature and the law-like nature of creation?

GUIDERDONI: That's right: regularities and continuous order. There is another very beautiful verse, which states that we shall not be able to find any "hole" in God's Creation; there are no defects. Everything is full of regularities and order. Because God Himself is order. God Himself is beauty. And the beauty that we see in the cosmos is an image of God's beauty.

This is the first point. The second point is that it's not surprising that these regularities are fundamentally intellectual. They are shaped by an Intelligence who also created our intelligence. So it is not surprising that we are able to explore the cosmos because it is not a foreign country. It is not different from us. We and the cosmos were created by the same Intelligence.

CLAYTON: Could this line of thinking lead toward a view of God's guidance of the world as involving not direct actions, but an original creation of an order that then characterizes the world at a later time? Or is it necessary to preserve continuing divine action?

GUIDERDONI: In Islamic theology there is something called the renewal of Creation at every moment. The argument is that the regularities present in the world are not existing *per se*; they could not be maintained if God was not there to create them anew at each moment. This idea has existed in Western philosophy also, under the name of "occasionalism." Islamic theology uses atomistic physics, so it could be, of course, rather close to our view of the cosmos, which is also atomistic. But the classical Ash'arite theology, which was developed during the ninth and tenth centuries, states that God creates the atoms and the accidents at each moment. So the atoms have no power of acting on other atoms simply because they don't have enough being. The causality is completely given by God. There is a classical example given by Imam al-Ghazali, one of the greatest Islamic thinkers. He says that fire by itself has no power to burn a piece of paper. If we bring fire close to a piece of paper, we see the paper burning, but this is not a consequence of putting the fire there. This is God's will because the fire by itself has not the capacity to burn. This is a strong statement and it is completely contrary to our way of seeing causality in the world. We can accept that God created the world with causality, with laws, but we have the feeling that after that Creation, God has left the laws to act in a mechanistic way. Classical Islamic theology states that, ultimately, the debate on causality is very complicated and is essentially metaphysical. Who makes natural laws? Are natural laws located in matter? Why are there natural laws at all? Newton would say that the law of gravitation is possible because God is present and maintains the law of gravitation at all times by its presence. Ultimately, I think Islamic theology is the same. The problems of causality and the permanence of the physical laws are central questions that have never been solved by our philosophy. Westerners tend to imagine the laws as an approximate description of the few regularities present in the world. In this view, matter would be dominated by cause and chance and we attempt to describe it in an approximate way. But in the theological view of Islam, the laws of nature are the "stuff" of the universe. The regularities, the symmetries, the laws of conservation, are our only description, our only way of thinking "matter," simply because matter is made from intellect. It is made with symmetry and mathematics.

CLAYTON: That's fascinating. Now let me move to a final, personal question, and ask you about the ways in which your religious belief has motivated your scientific work, if any, and the religious inspiration which you have drawn from your scientific research, or from astrophysics in general.

GUIDERDONI: Perhaps, a first step of any spiritual quest would be to be disappointed by some unanswered questions, and try to look for knowledge in another way: for instance, by going to Eastern countries, leaving behind all modern life and retiring to a monastery or an ashram. But that can be a way of denying reality. My religious practice has taught me that we have to accept reality as it is, with our limits. We have to live our life fully here, in the world, with all its limits, but also with all its beauty and richness. Science has many limits, but it has also great beauty and great interest. And this is the reason why I go on, and I hope I am going to improve myself in the future. But I see the two activities as converging toward the same reality.

6 Pauline Rudd
Molecular Grace

Pauline Rudd is a University Reader in Glycobiology at the University of Oxford. She has helped pioneer novel technologies for the rapid, sensitive analysis of sugars attached to glycoproteins. Most natural proteins contain sugars, and one aim of her research is to view glycoproteins as whole molecules, not just as proteins with bothersome sugars attached. Among other important functions, sugars on proteins play important roles in the immune system's ability to recognize antigens and thus defend the body from invasion. She has conducted basic research on the roles of sugars attached to glycoproteins involved in immunity, heart disease, rheumatoid arthritis, hepatitis, Creutzfeldt-Jakob disease and inflammation.

Rudd took fifteen years off from her research to raise four children, who are now aged from 23 to 34. She recently took a sabbatical from Oxford to work at the Scripps Research Institute in San Diego. In 1964, when studying Chemistry at London University, Rudd became a lay member of the Anglican Community of St Mary the Virgin in Wantage, Oxfordshire.

Science and religion are two different starting points from which we can explore different facets of the world and of ourselves, says Rudd. And the pursuits share much in common. Both require searching, rigorous honesty, discipline and austerity. "When I experience molecules," says Rudd, "it is a lot like how I experience God. I don't think of God as a person, but as something like the truth inside of me. So I don't have a visual picture of God, it's more an experiential picture. When I'm finally in tune with a molecule, I no longer have a visual picture of it, I have an experiential picture."

PAULINE RUDD: I am affiliated with the Anglican Church, the Church of England, and it has always been an integral part of me. I grew up in an Anglican home and as a small child I used religious language to express my experience. As I've grown older I've developed this use of religious symbolism and concepts. I haven't had any formal training, but just learned within the context of a normal church congregation by reading, discussing, writing and listening to people.

PHILIP CLAYTON: As you began studying at university and doing more advanced work in biology, did you experience conflicts between your religious perspective and your scientific work?

RUDD: At the end of my university days I had a very close association with a convent. I was drawn to it because I knew the people there understood how I felt. Because they were much more experienced in the religious life than I was they could affirm what was emerging in me and help me to grow in it. I considered that I might have a religious vocation. At that same time I was going out with an ordinand who was then priested and we were very much in love and obviously wanted to have children. In addition, when I was about thirteen I became committed to science, something I knew would last for the rest of my days. At age twenty, I had these three strands to my life that were all absolutely crucial. I went to the Mother Superior and she said that if I wanted to become a religious, I'd have to give up everything else. I went to my mother and she said if I wanted to have children, I'd have to give up everything else. And I talked to my professor and he said science would be all consuming. In those days – this was in the 1960s – if you were a woman and going to have a career in science you had to consider seriously whether you should have a family, and you certainly couldn't be a religious. Whatever I decided, two-thirds of me was going to be unfulfilled, so I went to the convent and became an Associate. Remarkably, they accepted a three-fold commitment. And so my whole life has been a living out of these three things. Sometimes I go deeper in one part. For example, the science may develop for a while at the expense of the others. But there's a point at which I can't go any further with science unless I understand the other facets of myself.

Because I am quite an intense and serious person, there are many things that I feel are important to pursue and I can't do them all at once – although I constantly try! Some things seemed to come into focus and I've needed to deal with them and understand them and then move on. But in the end, I can't live without all those three things. They've never been in conflict with each other, but sometimes my lack of maturity in one realm has prevented the development of another.

I've never experienced conflict between the content of my religion and my science. I never really accepted anything unless it correlated with my own understanding, so I didn't feel obliged to hold to any religious dogma that didn't seem relevant, or wasn't part of my present experience. As I grew, I simply evolved my religious practices and my religion to cope with my changing needs.

CLAYTON: How about the Bible?

RUDD: I don't think the Bible is necessarily literally true. It never seemed very reasonable or important to believe that the creation took place literally as it was written in the Bible, particularly since there are two versions. It's a mythology, a collection of writings, poetry, history, philosophical meandering. Religion for me is the part of the mythology I can relate to. At the greatest moments in my life I feel that I'm part of something that is ongoing. In what could be a very lonely universe I can find places where I feel I've got a foothold, because there's a mythology there which is relevant to my needs.

CLAYTON: Have you tried, wherever else your interpretations might have led you, to at least preserve the basic content of Christian ideas, or was everything a part of this on-going process of reflection and appropriation?

RUDD: Everything has been part of the process. Take the Creed for example. I remember as a teenager having trouble with the idea that Jesus descended into Hell, because the definition of Hell was where God was not. I reasoned that when Jesus descended there, God was there, so the statement was irrational. So I simply didn't say that bit in the Creed for a while, till I realized I was just being pedantic. Later, I understood that religion evolves. A lot of Christian beliefs are very, very ancient. To me that's what makes it special, actually: the idea of sacramental bread and wine goes back to the corn gods of Neolithic man. It's as if religion and Christianity have evolved with human thinking. And it continues to evolve with my thinking. That's part of what I think of as the inspiration of the Holy Spirit: the ability of each generation and each person to reinterpret for themselves, and to test what they believe. However, you can't just come to any outlandish conclusion uncritically; you do need to test what you find. If it's in direct contradiction to what other people say, you have to think again very hard, because you may be just going off arrogantly following your own fantasy. What's really important for me is to try to hold to my own integrity. If some commonly held doctrine helps you to understand what's going on in your life, then that's fine. But if it doesn't, the worst thing you can do is pretend that it does.

CLAYTON: Your attitude toward your religious belief is similar to the attitude of a scientist who sifts the data and accepts what she finds good reason to accept and feels a flexibility about traditional theories where they don't quite fit any longer.

RUDD: It is like science. God is very big. No one person and no one tradition, has it all together. In the end, I'm interested in what the real truth is. In science I don't have a preconceived idea of what I want – a piece of data or an experiment to show. I want to look at the data and then say, what is it telling me? It's exactly the same in my religious life.

If I don't understand something, or if I can't come to terms with something – either scientifically or by religious experience – I simply leave it as unresolved till either I have more life experience or something becomes clear. Often that does happen. There are some ideas in Christianity that I still don't understand, or that don't seem to matter to me, or to be important. But later in life something that seemed not to be important when I was younger may suddenly come into focus and really matter. For example, I found the suffering of Jesus on the cross very hard to understand until I suffered personally. Then it helped tremendously to know that God also understood about suffering and was alongside me.

CLAYTON: So, you're treating those bracketed-off parts of Christianity as metaphorical resources that may come alive and take on religious significance, meaning, or even truth, at the appropriate stage of your own development?

RUDD: Yes, and very often something just doesn't penetrate your thinking. You feel it is irrelevant because you don't understand where the person or text is coming from.

CLAYTON: Would that be a disanalogy with your practice as a scientist? Is it a difference between the subjective power of, say, the belief in Jesus's atoning death on the cross, on the one hand, and, on the other hand, a more objective question about a theory and whether a particular data set supports it?

RUDD: To some extent that's right. But the things that really excite me in science also spring from experience. I work with glycoproteins, which are very beautiful molecules. When I'm really familiar with a molecule, I actually feel that I'm inside of it. I can walk around it. It's huge and noisy and colored and got different patched areas. I even kind of understand how it feels and I know what it'll do if I put it into acid or into different situations. Also, there's always something about them that's still a mystery, which I still don't understand and I have to wait for more data, more to be revealed. Maybe there is a similarity with the way I feel about spiritual things. It is like the chemist Friedrich Kekule dreaming about a snake biting its own tail and realizing that that was a metaphor for the structure of the benzene ring.

CLAYTON: So the subjective/objective distinction doesn't really fit here, because science is not merely an objective, detached viewing of some phenomenon.

RUDD: Right, but science does have to be rational and so does religion. Intuition may take a big leap, but then, in science, you have to back it up with experiments. You must prove that your intuitive leap had some justification. In religion your intuitive leap may lead the intellect, and you may fill in the steps that got you there later, but in the end it has to be rational.

I'd like to be able to bring to science the kind of method and insights that I have in the realm of my religious and spiritual life. There's a close relationship between my unconscious experience and my conscious thinking in religion. Without too much difficulty I can bring my unconscious religious experience to a conscious articulation. I'd like to feel that I could also take my unconscious experience of a molecule and articulate it in scientific rationale and test it.

That's when I've made my greatest, most perceptive moves. But you can't just call it up to order. Those moments don't come very often and are very precious. Occasionally I have done it, but it's not normal procedure for me.

Articulating what we know on an unconscious level is vitally important. It frees your unconscious to go on and explore something else. Until you do that you can't really move on because your mind's still full of the clutter of the last unarticulated experience. With the base of articulated knowledge, you can search, like Theseus and the Minotaur and the thread held by Ariadne in the labyrinth in Crete. If you unwind the cord you can explore all over the place and can always bring the ideas or pieces of information that you've gleaned in your meandering back with you to your point of origin. You can come back to something you know you've rationally proved, where you are secure and can see how the new information that you're bringing back actually fits into that base. So to me, I suppose, it's a building of a secure place, a starting point and a place to always return to.

CLAYTON: A home.

RUDD: Yes, but nomadic, always changing. Never static because every time you come back you bring something new. In religion, if you approach it the way I have, it's quite dangerous because you could go off into some fantasy world. But if you always come back to where you've established a rational base, which you've tested with others, then I think you can afford to pursue things that are risky. What's right will come back and lock in, and stuff which is junk will fall away, just as in science.

CLAYTON: So our knowledge of the biological world and our religious beliefs serve as two different platforms, two different home bases in this domain we're exploring.

RUDD: Yes, but they are different. One's religion is exceedingly personal. No two people will ever put the puzzle together in the same order; everybody's personal situation is so different. But in science people do things in a similar order. You need to. Often you need one piece of information before you can get the next. Approaching molecules is in a sense much simpler. There aren't so many parameters.

CLAYTON: So in science the platform I return to is a communal one. Numerous people can read my articles and know what I've known and reconstruct it for themselves.

RUDD: Yes, and if they do the same scientific measurements, they'll obtain the same data. After a few years, people will agree on an interpretation. In the religious life it's nowhere near as simple. There may well never be a clear consensus.

CLAYTON: Earlier you said that I might appropriate religious beliefs but I could never test them in the same manner that I'll test a hunch in biochemistry.

RUDD: Not by physical measurement. But you can test against life experience. Religious experience either works or it doesn't, although it may be a while before you discover whether it works or not.

CLAYTON: So it's not as if I'm misunderstanding my religious beliefs if I say I'd like to test them against my life experience. I'm right to reject those that clash with my life experience and my intuitions.

RUDD: I don't accept anything in my religious faith unless it's come into focus. If people ask me if I believe in life after death, I say I don't know. I don't take someone else's idea from a book of dogma then try and test it. I build my faith from my own experience and spiritual life. For example, when I was a child I just couldn't accept the doctrine of the assumption. So I didn't include it in my own personal system of beliefs. It just sat there. Now my parents really wanted a boy, and from age three it was clear to me that it was a great advantage to be male. I heavily repressed the feminine side of myself. At around the time I had children I read Jung's discussion of Leonardo da Vinci's painting of the Madonna on the rocks. Here is the feminine stranded out on the rocks and abandoned, not relating to the rest of the psyche. I suddenly realized that this was what I had done to myself. Then I discovered the doctrine of the assumption, which, at a spiritual level, made it all make sense. In the doctrine of the assumption the feminine is part of the godhead, it's no longer just the three male things: Father, Son, Holy Spirit. Suddenly there's this recognizable feminine aspect of the godhead. It validated my own femininity, and I realized how important it is for the world and for women, to recognize the values of femininity. So now, because of that, the doctrine of the assumption is important to me.

CLAYTON: Do you believe in a personal God?

RUDD: Yes, yes.

CLAYTON: Is Christ for you somehow a special manifestation of God, or the manifestation of God in human flesh?

RUDD: Well, I believe that all of us are born with a life spark within us, which I call God, the deepest root and ground of my being. I think all of us to some extent display that in our inner life. But for many of us it's very clouded because we haven't got the courage, or we're not really that in touch with that part of ourselves. I think Jesus was somebody for whom there was not so much of a barrier between the inner and the outer person. He was able to show that divine spark with all its beauty and majesty in a way that no other person has been able to do. That's part of how I understand the incarnation and what I understand about Jesus.

CLAYTON: Would you understand in a similar way traditional beliefs such as sin, separation from God and Christ's redemptive work as making the way open again between humanity and God?

RUDD: The idea of the God who dies for his people is very ancient and in some ways the ultimate expression of love. I think Jesus came at a point in history where all those things made sense to the people around him. However, I have difficulty with the idea of somebody dying for my sins. I just don't want to dump the responsibility onto somebody else. Also, I have children, and as Kierkegaard explored in *Fear and Trembling*, I don't see that sacrificing one of my children in that way would be an honorable thing to do. I can only approach this idea through mythology. I do think that the kind of life Jesus lived is inevitably going to end up in some kind of sacrifice. Christ's was an uncomfortable and inconvenient way of life and, in the end, if you keep your integrity and keep to the truth, you'll probably end up dead because the rest of the world can't handle it.

I have trouble with the question, "Are you saved?" I've always believed that God loves me as I am. I don't have to pretend to be anything other. The motivation for not sinning is the pain of being separated from the light that's within you. You don't want to do anything to disturb that. It's crucial to your well-being. So God in a sense lifts you up – the presence of God is actually what saves you, not the death of somebody. Maybe I understand the significance of the death of Christ a little more now that I am older. However, what's important to me is the idea that mankind was taken into the godhead rather than that God came to man. God was already in man, because He created man. The point is that He took man into Himself, like at the Ascension. He actually raised man up to have aspirations that were far beyond his wildest dreams. In doing that, sin kind of fluffs away because the longing to have what is so much more valuable shows the lesser things to be just entanglements.

CLAYTON: You see sin as a separation from God?

RUDD: A separation from the life-giving part of myself, yes. There are some things we all agree are sin, but even then we make exceptions. For example, we say, "Thou shalt not murder – except in a war," which we justify by making a distinction between murdering and killing. It's very difficult to know intellectually what sin is, but you do know spiritually because sin is what disturbs your inner peace.

CLAYTON: What about the traditional belief in a purpose or destiny or telos for the universe? Is this compatible with the conclusions of biology?

RUDD: Well, the idea that the universe is an expression of the love of God, the mind of God, or the expressed word of God makes sense to me. I don't think the universe is just blind chaos, just the product of combinations of molecules – I mean these molecules have organized themselves into man who is able to reflect on himself and reflect on the universe, and in some sense create his own idea of God. And I think that God is at the very least as great as the sum total of mankind!

I don't know about destiny. I would go along with St Paul that creation is groaning and struggling to become more perfect, whatever that means. In the heart of most people is a desire to reach some ideal of justice and peace, of care for each other, of leaving the worst side of human relationships behind us, trying to move toward something Christians might call the Kingdom of God. If God is at the heart of all people and if collectively we are in some sense the mind of God, then there is some destiny because we all try to move towards one for ourselves, don't we? We try to reach some end point in our lives and to have something meaningful to say at the end of them. And I suppose the sum total of all that adds up to a destiny for mankind.

CLAYTON: Theologians seem to be divided nowadays between the traditional view and something like an Augustinian view, where God stands outside of the physical universe. Since time is a physical phenomenon, God would be timeless. Others seem to speak of God more in terms of process, as being involved in the process of the unfolding of the universe and the evolution of life and as guiding humanity and so forth.

RUDD: My view is that God is immanent and intimately concerned with every part of humanity. The other thing that's really important to me is cooperation with God. I think we have the responsibility for working with God to decide when we have children, for example, and we have the responsibility to work with God in how we bring those children up. It's not as if God pulls puppet strings or has some idea that we haven't bought into. It's a cooperative process, for me anyway. The universe evolves by the way nature selects itself, and by the way man interacts with nature, and how individual men are inspired by their understanding of God to move things in that direction. But that's a very limited view, isn't it? There's also the transcendent God of the cosmos, and, I suppose, of the Big Bang and the controler of the major events of the universe, and I don't understand much about Him.

CLAYTON: But you do feel that the God who cooperates with us here at this level also operates at the level of cosmology?

RUDD: I would imagine, yes. If God can identify with me, He can identify with a molecule or the universe, can't He? Or if I can identify with a molecule, certainly God can, but I don't have any inside information about what the direction is, and it doesn't worry me particularly. Science and religion say the same things; the universe will have a beginning and it will have an end, and then maybe it will re-emerge. But I find it difficult to believe that there's a person up there directing it all, or pre-planning it. That just takes away the really magnificent thing about humankind, that we do have some measure of control, and we do have some responsibility. If you believe that everything's predestined and it doesn't matter what you do – well, nothing really matters. Paul Tillich's book, *The Courage to Be*, comes to mind. Part of the greatness of being human is that you have the courage to go on and have dreams, that we still believe that it's worth being just and honorable, even though we know that the sun and the solar system will one day not be here and it won't really matter. The fact that we have the courage to continue in light of this is some indication of the greatness of the created world, isn't it?

CLAYTON: So you don't find any incompatibility between the physicist's account of how the earth got here up to the moment of the first self-reproducing cell and the religious account that says God was directing that process.

RUDD: How do we know? I mean, all I am sure about is that I experience a God who really cares, who interacts with me personally and with the world. If people are killed in a natural disaster, He is there suffering with them. One of my children is in a wheelchair. When that happened, I was convinced that God was not just allowing it to happen and not caring, but that He was suffering with us. There's a natural world that has its own laws. Maybe God intervenes, but I don't understand why He should create a world and then interfere in the natural creation as though He had got it wrong in the first place. I have trouble with that.

I don't know what will happen when I die. But I do believe, or feel, or know, that the God who has loved and cared and interacted with me since before I was old enough to put a name to it will continue to do that after I die. I don't need to know any more than that.

CLAYTON: And the same thing would presumably be true of history on a much larger scale?

RUDD: Well, as we learn more about it we may begin to see patterns that look like destiny. That would be very interesting. But I don't have preconceived ideas that would be threatened if science found it one way or the other.

CLAYTON: Christianity emphasizes the person's special qualities of freedom and moral responsibility and his or her capacity for relationship with God. Does knowledge about our evolutionary history in any way threaten this notion of the person as free and morally responsible before God?

RUDD: Biology doesn't attempt to address that, does it? Most people feel that they are individuals, and they do have responsibility, and they do have free choices. I was thinking about this the other day, and I haven't quite thought this through, but if something is a simple and dependable process, there's generally only one way of doing it. For example, all mammals use hemoglobin to take up oxygen by the red cells. It's quite a simple thing and it only happens in one mechanistic way.

On the other hand, complex organisms like humans need to have free choice to be adaptable to a huge variety of circumstances. One way of structuring your community may be fine when the weather's dry, but if you suddenly get flooded out in Bangladesh, then you have to re-organize very quickly and re-group. And that requires conscious choice. Unconsciously reacting to your genes certainly wouldn't give you the same kind of flexibility that thinking out various possibilities would.

I think biology and evolution explain a great deal. They help us to understand many of the things we do. But I don't think they're adequate to explain the whole system of checks and balances and human altruism. I was just reading Primo Levi's accounts of the concentration camps, where people gave things to others although they were depriving themselves of something which may have been life-giving for them. Why would human beings spend time painting? It's not essential to survival. Why aren't we just sort of functional food seekers? Why do we live beyond our reproductive years? Biology would have to propose the species' purpose in rather bold detail for it to convince me that we are only responding to biological stimuli all the time. Maybe something deeper inspires the firing of the synapses. I suppose that, without any real evidence, I feel that a human is more than the sum total of biological parts, just as I feel that God is far more than the expressions of God in us. And community is like that, isn't it? It's more than the sum total of the individuals. It has a life of its own, and a crowd of people becomes an organism, which is the sum total of all the people within it, but it also has something beyond and even above that. Perhaps it's like playing a musical instrument. You play all the notes but when they make a tune it's actually something beyond the sum total of the notes, and something comes out from it that has meaning and expression, which is far beyond the notes on the page, or the individual notes made by the musician. I suppose I think a human being's like that. None of that goes with wanting to survive at all costs and not caring about anybody else.

As for the uniqueness of humans, I do think that we're the only species that can reflect upon itself. We also have much greater powers to articulate and to communicate abstract ideas.

CLAYTON: Some philosophers of biology speak about "emergent properties." Life, they might say, is an emergent property of complicated molecular structures, right? A soul does things that can only be explained in terms of a soul. A cell does things that can only be explained in biological terms; no amount of chemistry is going to explain its behaviors. Then, at the upper end of biological development, we see emergent properties of the brain, namely, thoughts, which are more than synaptic firings and which require a new explanatory vocabulary.

RUDD: Yes, you've said it more eloquently and much more succinctly. I think that's really lovely, actually, that just makes sense to me. And I think the spiritual emerges from the lower levels. The traditional doctrine says that Jesus is wholly man and wholly God. I think that is the emergence of man into the godhead. The ability to experience a spiritual dimension grows out of being human and in a sense it's an encounter experience. Something almost like a dream emerges; it has no words and isn't articulated, and you then articulate that, and it becomes a spiritual reality to you and then you simply build on this emerging life experience. Or your spiritual growth constantly allows this soul, or whatever I am, to develop.

CLAYTON: Christianity holds that God is present and active in the world, a source of purpose, a giver of freedom and this spiritual dimension. Some people claim that our increased knowledge of the world leaves less room for any direct divine action, that we simply don't see any sign now that we know so much about physical law, and so much about biology. What do you think?

RUDD: In the past people thought that God directed the floods of the Nile or caused pestilence. We don't think that way any more. But each generation has its own needs and interprets religion for its own time. I'm very aware of the presence of God, not necessarily directing anything but being there to meet me when I need to grow. I see God as something very strong requiring the best from me. It is more like that than the idea of a God that comes in miraculously to solve problems.

CLAYTON: You put more emphasis on something experienced at the personal level, on one's awareness of herself and her hopes and her ambitions and her moral responses.

RUDD: Yes. One place where I find God is at those times in life where the way I'm living is no longer appropriate, either because I've matured or because circumstances around me have changed and I need to fall apart and then re-assess and re-assemble. I look within myself for resources that I've never used before, because I've never been in that situation before. For instance, when my children left home I suddenly had another part of life in front of me, and I needed to re-assess and re-think and look within myself, trying to find signposts. I do have a lot of helpful dreams, and I think then I am searching my subconscious for guidance or signposts and that's where I meet God. And for each generation those challenges and those things will be different.

CLAYTON: So it's a misunderstanding to say that I can trust God to alter natural events so that, let's say, my children will be protected on their way to school?

RUDD: For me, the divine role is that, whatever happens, God will support you and enable you to handle it. You can look to God as a resource to giving you the courage you need to cope with whatever life turns up. But clearly God doesn't work unnatural miracles. Sometimes things happen which you may interpret as miraculous, but I don't believe that God operates that way.

CLAYTON: Do you derive religious inspiration, in the sense that we've been talking about, from your scientific work?

RUDD: When I write creatively about my spiritual development I often use scientific metaphors. For example, I remember writing about my relationship with God being like DNA, twisted but then separating. So I've certainly used things from science, but I also think that when I experience molecules, it is a lot like how I experience God. I don't think of God as a person, but as something like the truth inside of me. So I don't have a visual picture of God; it's more an experiential picture. When I'm finally in tune with a molecule, I no longer have a visual picture of it, I have an experiential picture. I'm sometimes drawn into a scientific contemplative state, which is very similar to a contemplative religious state. It's not visual, I'm not imagining it in my mind and I'm not talking to it in my mind, I'm actually contemplatively experiencing it.

CLAYTON: Does your practice on the one side lead to greater depth or adeptness on the other?

RUDD: I don't think that that kind of contemplative state is something I've learned. It's something that I've always known. It's a natural way of being for me. However, there are things that go along with being contemplative that at the deepest level also apply to science. Discipline and austerity are important. It should be like looking at a tree without leaves in winter; just the bare essentials and no pretence and no trying to imagine it's what you'd like it to be. That's crucial in religion and spiritual development. Of course that's also crucial in science. In that sense I do take what I've learned from my religious tradition into science, and certainly the other way around.

And part of being human for me is trying to reach the unknowable, both in science and religiously within myself. It's like the story of Parsifal. He tasted the salmon and then dropped it because it was too hot to handle and he couldn't interpret it. But for the rest of his life he searched to repeat that experience. It was so precious. That's where I am with religion. Once you've been touched, then it's so desirable that you'll sacrifice almost anything else to understand more and to experience more.

CLAYTON: You said that the development of reason on the scientific side has allowed you think about religion in a richer way, and that the development of intuition or contemplation has contributed not only to your scientific discoveries, but to the creative process of writing about them so that there's been a positive cross-fertilization between these areas.

RUDD: Yes, yes, there's been a huge amount of cross-fertilization. And all of it stems from love. The response that I had to science when I was thirteen was purely one of the heart, and so of course is my life with my family characterized by love, just as my response to God and the desire to follow a religious vocation is one of the heart. Although the intellect and its analysis follows quite quickly, the initial response is from the heart. It wasn't that I sought God, but that He sought me. It wasn't that I sought chemistry, but chemistry sought me, and when I came in contact with it, something inside me leapt and recognized that that's where I wanted to be, where I belonged.

7   Mark Pesce
Virtually Sacred

Researcher, author and radical theorist Mark Pesce was the Principal Engineer for Shiva Corporation, the company credited with inventing dial-up networking. In 1994, Pesce and his collaborator Tony Parisi developed a virtual interface to the World Wide Web that became the basis for the Virtual Reality Modeling Language (VRML), which has since grown into the standard interface technology for virtual reality on the World Wide Web. Pesce was the founding Chair of the University of Southern California's School of Cinema-Television's Interactive Media Program and is the author of three books on new technology. His most recent book, *The Playful World: How Technology is Transforming our Imagination*, examines the role of play in education, the emerging world of high-tech toys, and the ability of play to form and transform human consciousness.

His work with virtual reality has made Pesce extra sensitive to the medium's incredible potential, both for good and for harm. Until now, the ordinary and identifiable interfaces to perception have protected people from the mainlining of the intentions of others, but they also made impossible direct forms of interpersonal and artistic communication. As studies in virtual reality identify and evade those interfaces, what Pesce calls the FX boundaries, the opportunities for beneficial communication leaps as do the potentials for nefarious dominance.

Pesce directs his spiritual practice of witchcraft toward imbuing the new technologies he creates with life-enhancing powers, rather than life-negating ones. He cites Marshall McLuhan's view that while new technologies enhance some human capacities they amputate others, reconfiguring the nature of the person who employs them. In this sense, Pesce says, the technologies we develop and the ways we develop them will shape the course of human evolution. The big question then is, how do we do this in a sacred way, not a profane one?

MARK PESCE: I was raised Catholic. In my late teens I went through a classic conversion experience, à la William James, into Pentecostal Protestantism. That lasted for about a year and a half. After that, I shied away from almost any sort of religious involvement at all until I was very nearly thirty years old, when I started to understand my own experience and to conceptualize it into terms that are probably familiarly called paganism. I try not to name it, because I think it is much more a melange of a lot of different religious traditions, including Christian, pre-Christian, Buddhist, Taoist and so on. As for my regular, specific religious practice, it is a witchcraft, or pagan practice. But I still see myself as very syncretic with the other traditions.

GORDY SLACK: What are the fundamentals of the witchcraft tradition?

PESCE: My own understanding is that the pagan, or pre-Christian, traditions focus on the essential harmony between the self, our being and the universe. And this is practiced by harmonizing yourself with the cycle of time. The pagan practice, the practice of witchcraft, is about knowing what time it is, and, from that, being able to deduce what things are appropriate to the moment. There is a very regular annual cycle, sometimes called the cycle of the Wheel in the Craft traditions. The begin date is actually this Friday – which would be called Halloween in the more profane tradition – Samhain is what it is called in the pagan tradition. It is a cycle of death, birth and death again. It flows very naturally from the seasons, which is where it was originally derived. There is an encapsulation into mythology of the natural forms, and if you harmonize with these natural forms, you stay in harmony not only with yourself, but with the world around you. In that sense, paganism is a practice of harmony, a religion of harmony with yourself and the environment.

SLACK: Remember that hip-hop fashion in the eighties of wearing a big clock around your neck? The other day I heard a musician saying that that was about letting people know that you knew what time it was. As the eighties progressed the clocks on the necklaces got bigger and bigger. The obvious question for you now is, from a pagan point of view, what time is it? And how does technology, and the work you do with VRML in particular, fit into this time?

PESCE: It is time to put aside mechanistic conceptions of the universe and mechanistic conceptions of the self. Or rather, it's time to augment the mechanistic understanding of the self with a broader understanding of both the self and the universe. It's time to see things in wholes. When I started working in virtual reality, which was back pretty much when the field was starting, I had no philosophical frame for understanding my work's significance. After I'd been working for a number of years, I started to understand not just the physics of virtual reality, but also some of the metaphysics and psychology of the virtual world. A lot of this came from my having digested people like Marshall McLuhan, who had a theory about media which, as far as I can tell, proves itself most truthfully in virtual media. He said that technologies act as amputations. In order to use a technology, you have to supplant some innate function of yourself. A car is a very good example. In order to operate one, you have to supplant the natural function of the legs, which is locomotion, and replace it with a control interface, that is, the pedals, the steering wheel and so on. But with that amputation you give yourself a greater ability. There is always this element of closing off some innate ability in order to augment ability. Well, fine, we can gain a lot of facility by doing that. However, we also change our own interior landscape. We change our psychology. All organisms, when they are functioning within larger environments, exchange information with the environments around them. When they do this, they enter into what are called structural couplings. You could almost think of them as feedback loops between the organism and the environment. And then these structural couplings create new coherent entities. In other words, you can't decouple the organism from the environment it's in. You have to consider it as a whole.

So any technology that we adapt to we also incorporate, both physically and into our ontology. And that's a very important point. Now, the thing about virtual technologies is that they are complete in their abilities to amputate innate experience.

If we posit a hypothetical state of complete immersion in a virtual world, we have supplanted all the natural sensoria with artificial sensoria. Then there is a structural coupling to a world that is artificial in manufacture. What then becomes of imminent importance is the intent of the creator of that construction.

SLACK: There is the intent and there is the effect, and they may not be the same.

PESCE: Intent cannot deterministically set effect, but it can induce structural couplings, which will produce some effects. So the intent of the designer becomes increasingly important, and in fact becomes of paramount importance in the sense that the unity that can be formed creates a very powerful conduit for information into the self.

All right, let's take another step back. I'm trying to give you all the threads and show you how they lead into one point. In a radical branch of psychology known as "neurocosmology," the entire universe is divided into three fields of information. There is everything outside of you, and we will label that with the Greek letter Phi for the physical world. There is everything inside of you – your thoughts, your emotions, your feelings – we will label that Psi for the psychic realm. Then there is everything that is in between, because there is no excluded middle in this theory. And we'll call that FX, and those are the sensors and affectors by which the outside world gets in and the inside world gets out. It's not important to identify what's in any of these realms. What's important to identify are the boundaries that exist between them, because the physical world can't manifest itself directly into the psychic world, but has to pass through this biological layer, or what William Gibson in *Neuromancer* would have called "the meat." And the same thing is true for messages emanating from the self.

They have to pass through. So the boundaries, then, indicate the areas of importance.

Information is always lost at these boundaries. For example, if I were to take an infrared remote control for a television set and flash it at you, well, there is information coming out of the device, but you don't perceive it because you aren't sensually equipped for it. Information is being lost at the boundary between the physical world and your biology. On the other hand, if I were to say *watashi wa midori no chisai no hito desu*, (Japanese for, "I am a little green man"), information might be lost between your biology and your cognitive self. If you're Japanese you have an innate interface to this information so that it can go from the physical world into the world of your self. But if you don't know Japanese, then that information gets filtered away as noise in the FX/Psi boundary.

SLACK: So there are different layers to the FX/Psi boundary.

PESCE: Right, and those layers can be trained. We call that learning. If I gave you a set of infrared goggles then you'd be able to see the remote quite clearly. So we have techniques and tools for bridging those boundaries. The essence of virtual reality is learning the structure of those boundaries and how to bridge them. We are moving toward a condition where the physical world can be represented with perfect fidelity in the internal world. That raises a very important point, because at the time that you can do that you have created a cyborg.

So we're talking about closing off the facility of human consciousness, which allows for ambiguity and interpretation in its signals. This is a fecund ground for creativity. But creating machines that faithfully represent also poses an enormous danger. We are stumbling around in this area. Some people will be doing so with the conscious intent to reinforce the innate being of the self – the artist Char Davies is a very good instance of that. Other people would be working with a conscious intent to use technology pathologically, to destroy the innate abilities of the self, or to refigure them in ways that the self may not want. That raises serious ethical issues and everything that I do in my work is tinged with that ethical quality. On the one hand, I have created a great tool for communication. On the other hand, I've helped to create a great tool for domination. That's the pallor cast over my entire work. I've tried to take a look at what can induce vivo-genic, or healthful, states in the communion with these artifacts.

I start from Mircea Eliade's statement in *The Sacred and the Profane*, that "The sacred is that which ontologically founds the world." In other words, the place for being, and that includes human being, is provided for by the creation of a place for the sacred. That serves as the foundation and justification for all of my work. It's an attempt to unite technology with elements of the sacred.

SLACK: By "that which ontologically founds the world" do you mean "reality"?

PESCE: Yes, and that goes for any world, whether it is a real world or a virtual world. It makes no difference. I think in an onto-logical sense, you get onto very slippery ground when you start to say this is real and this is virtual. Let me give you an example of what I'm talking about. The first time I attempted a unification of these realms was when we were just getting started on our work in VRML. This was also during my first year of serious study of witchcraft. Witchcraft is essentially an oral tradition. There are books, but essentially it is passed down from teacher to student. And in that sense, there is a lot of practice, there is a lot of information, there is a lot of just hanging out with the teacher in order to understand the way they work. It's not pre-eminently a rational mode. It's pre-eminently an intuitive mode. You have to understand the being of the teacher and how they approach the subject of their belief rather than just mouthing words. I'd been practicing pretty steadily for a year and it was time for what is called, in witchcraft terms, my first degree. That's when you've learned enough that the training wheels can be taken off the bike and you can actually do a ritual yourself. I wanted to conceptualize how VRML could be used to create a sacred space, a space in which a human being could reflect his or her own sacred nature. From this I conceptualized what I called the CyberSamhain, which happened three years ago yesterday. The CyberSamhain was a ritual held simultaneously in cyberspace and in real space. We used VRML to model a sacred circle, and a sacred circle in witchcraft is constructed out of the four directions: the East is earth, the South is fire, the West is water and the North is air. We created an altar with things representing the Goddess and the God and had that space linked and available across the World Wide Web, which was still very much in its infancy at that point. Anyone who wanted to could join us in the ritual on the web, or in real space. This was covered in some detail in *Wired* [issue 3. 07].

I was the facilitating force for the ritual, but I did not compose it all. Instead, I went to several of my friends who were also practicing these traditions, and assigned them roles. I said, "I want you to write your own part in this and the only guideline I have is that it should rhyme." Together these contributions created what I would call an emergent ritual form. In other words, the parts came together into a coherent whole because each part independently was intelligent enough and free enough to be able to gather and integrate. I was attempting to represent how I saw the Web forming and how I saw the Internet forming, as a self-organizing system of intelligent parts coming together to create a whole. This also embodies my own understanding of how the magical universe works.

As near as anyone can tell, the ritual was successful at creating a sacred space. It was the ritual of Samhain, the ritual of the dying of the God. It is the entity that dies and enters the shadow realm. One of the philosophical arguments I was making at that point was that there is no fundamental difference between the virtual world and the shadow realm, in other words, the Dreamtime. And what I wanted to do was to say, "Okay, if the God is in the Shadow, he can also be in the Dreamtime of cyberspace." So the ritual was welcoming the God into cyberspace.

And I've had very good computer juju since then; I don't know whether or not that's related. I don't want to invoke any degree of causality – but that was when we saw VRML and the Web take off rapidly.

If we are in relation to our machinery, then our machinery is affecting us. If we don't bless the machinery, if we don't imbue it with the sacred, then it will invariably profane us. There is no option there. And so the idea was to imbue that spirit into the machinery. To say, okay, well, this machinery is artifact as much as any of our artifacts. We choose to bless artifacts in the real world so that we can remember the sacred when we interact with them, let's do the same thing with this.

SLACK: In Bali there's a day set aside each year for blessing tools. People take out their hoes and scissors and kitchen tools and thank them and make offerings to them.

PESCE: Right. And that's exactly it. It's to remember that all work in some sense is sacred work. All things that you form should be imbued with the image of the sacred. And so I saw this ritual in a philosophical frame or a religious frame as a good thing to do. But I also did it because of my understanding of the effect of artifact on psychology as being a necessary thing to do, in other words, a protective measure. A prophylactic.

SLACK: I hope it works.

PESCE: Well, it needs to be repeated every year. And when I'm bringing up a new website, before it goes public I put a page of invocation and blessing on its root page. I know, then, that I have, through my own will, done my best to realize the sacred ambition for it.

I think that mainstream Protestant culture is very disconnected from artifact in that sense, as are, I suppose, the Islamic and Jewish cultures. They each have a strong abhorrence of the image. But the pagan cultures, the Hindu cultures, the other cultures have a very great deal of respect for that form of blessing.

SLACK: Is it possible to identify with any precision at all where the FX/Psi boundary is? Is it really at the surface of the eye, the surface of the body? If, as you say, VR is about identifying that boundary and learning how to penetrate or bridge it—

PESCE: Done pathologically it's about penetration. Done in a manner of consummation, then that's bridging it.

SLACK: Okay, then how to bridge it. Could you say more about the nature of that boundary? You're suggesting that it is not definite?

PESCE: Absolutely. There are certain boundaries to expressiveness that we know exist. This is why we resort to music, or to painting, or to ballet. Because they bridge boundaries in expression that we normally linguistically have a great deal of trouble with. In that sense, I see VR as having some facility that exists above and beyond normal language, but if you are asking me where I'm going to locate the real and the virtual, yeah, you are right. A cognitive psychologist would tell us that about 99 percent of all of our experience is being generated in our brain anyway, and all of the rest is memory and supposition.

SLACK: Where does that leave you in developing VRML?

PESCE: A few years ago I saw something that totally twisted my mind in a beautiful way. It was a piece called T_Vision. It's a visualization system that runs on a big SGI supercomputer and it shows you a high-resolution image of the Earth as it is right now. It uses a network of satellites and other systems, and they are all collating and collecting data. And you can surf the Earth's surface in real time. It's an incredible piece of work. I used that as an archetype to design a scaled down version, which I called WebEarth [www.webearth.org], which I built out of VRML using real-time satellite images. This means that everyone on their desktop can now have an image of the Earth as it is floating in space. We are creating a structural coupling between those kinds of systems and ourselves, wherein we start to blur the boundary between the human biota and the Gaian biota. In other words, we can now start to see the loops in ecology to understand the affect of our own actions on our environment. That, to me, reinforces the natural tendency toward life. And so that's become one focus of my own work.

I've also started a company to do web entertainment using VRML. This is in part a reaction to the fact that I think the Web right now is a humorless medium. It hasn't sufficiently incorporated the human capacity to laugh or to cry.

SLACK: Will adding another dimension to cyberspace make it more humorous?

PESCE: The fidelity of computing in general has been on the increase since its beginnings – since it began with a one-dimensional command line, then went to a two-dimensional graphical computer interface, and now three and four dimensions, into both 3-D modeling and virtual reality. Each of these are about sensualizing the interface, which is the key to being emotionally affective and affective at other levels that are not normally thought of as the facility of computing, but are thought of as the facility of human communication. I'm saying that Web isn't about computer communication, it's about human communication. It's about being able to get us to each other through it.

SLACK: Through to each other and also to the foundation for the sacred, which may not be another person, but may be a thing, say the planet Earth, seen hurtling through space.

PESCE: Exactly. It can be lots of different things. People always ask me what the sacred is and I always get very fuzzy on that point. But as a guideline, I would say that the sacred is that which reinforces the vitality of that which it encounters.

SLACK: I'd like to switch gears here for a second. The religious or spiritual interpretation of life often implies a very definite sense of purpose to human experience and to the way things unfold. Yet a lot of twentieth-century science looks at the universe as the result of not an intention, God's intention or Gaia's intention, or whatever, but rather as the unfolding of a non-intentional chain of events. How would you frame this debate, and where do you fall in it?

PESCE: I think that Teilhard de Chardin's idea of a teleological gathering and complexification in systems – that things will gather to a certain point of external complexity and then they will turn that complexification inward – is a useful model for understanding the processes that are proceeding on the planet. He implies that there is a divine Telos that is guiding that – the Omega. I will remain silent on that, because it matters less if it's literally true than if it's functionally true. In other words, are we working within that milieu? I think that the neogenesis of the Web represents a concrete physical manifestation of a force that we can't see – because we are embedded in it – but that is directing us to its own ends. The Web appeared simultaneously and ubiquitously. This is the first technology to do that in the history of human culture. It self creates, but it uses us as the agent of that self creation. It puts us into a feedback loop with respect to it, invoking its own self into being. So I look at that and I say, "Okay, there is the footprint in the sand." I don't know what the beast is that made that foot-print, but I can presume, because I see the footprint, that there is some thing that is making it.

SLACK: Daniel Dennett talks about religious explanation as a kind of "skyhook," where the "force" is teleological, it comes from God up above reaching down and pulling culture, history, natural history, whatever, into the future along a road laid down by His intentions. Evolutionists try very, very hard to find other explanations, that is, to explain how these things proceed moved from below.

PESCE: If you locate God in the Gaian body, then you locate it below.

SLACK: But is Mark Pesce's universe an inherently purposeful place where things happen for a reason, or reasons, or is the purpose we see in it normative, generated by our interpreta-tion of it?

PESCE: Well, there is something happening here that we are a part of. Of that I am absolutely sure. Whether it's coming from above or below, I think a lot of that depends on your point of view. I could adopt either point of view, depending on which frame I'm working in. And I don't find them exclusionary. I'm not trapped in the essential paradox of that because I do see the Gaian bios as being alive. I think that the human destiny within it is to act as stewards. As the conscious entity on this planet, our job is to manage not only our world, but the entire planet as self-consciously as we can, and to try to have as little impact on the overall biosphere as possible. And that conviction certainly influences the direction of a lot of my work.

So, I would choose a teleology that is personal to me. That's the teleology that's most resonant with where I see myself in the grander scheme of things.

SLACK: Do you think that the self-organizing entities emerging from the digital world will be anything like human beings? Will there be emergent properties that will be justifiably called "persons" that will be based on a different biology? And if so, how does this shift things ethically? And how does it fit into Teilhard's teleology?

PESCE: The body serves not only as the vehicle for the mind, but the mind and the body play together. They are two fields that are interacting to produce the person. The closest thing I have to a personal eschatology would be derived both from the pagan traditions and from the Buddhist traditions. I believe there is some "beingness" that is immanent and permanent and that survives the death of the physical vehicle. I think that if we are talking about a field of what the Buddhists would call mind, then mind manifests itself in a physical being, interacts with it, is changed by it and so on. In a sense, the body "is" so that mind can enter time and can project itself through time and so that mind can actually change.

Now that body doesn't have to be like our own, but if it's not, then the manifestation of consciousness that arises in it will not be like our own. So if we are talking about machine consciousness, my own feeling is that such a thing can exist. I'm not sure, though, if we should expect to communicate with it in a meaningful way. The only way to do that would be to give it a form which is in some sense similar to our own.

SLACK: Are you describing something like Cog, which is a robot they are creating at MIT at the AI Lab? They are trying to create a "baby" that has as many human properties and human-like experiences as possible. They will nurture it in the hope that it will develop attachments and so forth.

PESCE: That represents one valid approach. Otherwise, we'll get forms so alien that any meaningful form of interaction may be impossible. On the other hand, maybe it will be so alien that the interactions will be intensely meaningful. It introduces a very interesting set of boundaries, because it's the created rather than the born, and it will introduce a very interesting set of structural couplings between ourselves and it, especially because I do not think we will be responsible for investing it with consciousness. I think we will be responsible for investing it with the place that consciousness can be manifested in it.

SLACK: But where will the responsibility for a cyborg's consciousness lie if not with us?

PESCE: We have a responsibility to nurture it. But if conscious entities possess free will – and I know this has been debated endlessly – then responsibility will ultimately lie within the entity.

I find the regions of cyberspace ontologically identical to magical space. One of the elements of magical space is an ontology that is conformant to will. When I take a look at that and I take a look at the technological endpoints we seem to be racing towards – and when I say that I mean nanotechnology and fully realized cyberspace – that also is a world conformed to will. So I see the technological impulses having the same natural arc as my practice of Craft. And I think that my practice of Craft is serving to inform those impulses which, by themselves, devoid of any manifest sacred presence, could become malevolent, could become pathological.

SLACK: Right. The medium by its nature is imbued with will. But that which you will determines whether it can be good or not.

PESCE: Right, exactly. And the supreme rede in Craft is that "Love is the Law." And it's similar to the Buddhist tradition of compassion and the Christian practice of love. "Love is the Law" informs the arc.

SLACK: Say more about the dangers you've mentioned. And does your practice of Craft give you ethical imperatives, or instructions, about resisting them? Ritual is one kind of action, but are there others?

PESCE: The danger is that the technology will produce manifestations that are pathogenic. And nanotechnology is a very clear case of the problem that represents this sort of entropic dwell state, where everything gets melted down into the big sea of gray goo. With the construction of a nanite whose only imperative is replication, the Earth's surface would be reduced to copies of the nanite – gray goo – in about 72 hours. We don't want that. So it has to, in some sense, inform my work. As for my work in cyberspace, it's about creating ways to be able to manifest the sacred self and to be able to communicate the "beingness" of that sacred self. My work in planetary visualization and in systems like that is another reflection. Since I can't change anyone but myself, all I can do is produce forms that illustrate my own particular view of things. Witchcraft is very clear on the question of will. Each of us has his own will and everyone else has their own will, and you can't do anything about that. You can't effectively influence another person.

Witchcraft is about cleansing the self, because only from that position can you do anything in the world. Once you've done that, or once you're on that path, then what will happen ideally, is that other people will see and learn from the examples you create.

This feeds back into chaos theory; sensitive dependence on initial conditions. When VRML was starting up I saw the opportunity and the need to produce commanding examples of the work to show how it could be used for positive purposes. This could produce an environment where positive purposes would be more likely to be realized. And I think that's it. You have to have humility about how much you can change the world or change others.

SLACK: But in dealing with a technology that is as contagious as this, and when you're at the hub of innovation and influence, you don't want to underestimate how much you affect things.

PESCE: Well, you can choose to be frightened. And if you do, then you'll just fall into inaction. I don't choose to be frightened so much as I choose to be fully informed and to fully inform others of the dangers. If people understand the consequences of their actions, then their actions themselves will be mitigated in that light.

Will shapes perception and perception shapes reality. I have studied under teachers who have done their best to show me the truth of this statement, and, as I grow older – and hopefully wiser – I come to see it more and more clearly: "We are pan-dimensional wizards, casting arcane spells with every word we speak, and all our spells always come true." This was a fragment of knowledge I received early on, but it took me some years before I understood it at all. I'm still working on it.

There's another truth, for those who can receive it. You are your own High Priest. You mediate your own relationship to the divine; no one else can assume that role – though many try constantly. When one is ready to accept this as truth, one is open to a relationship with divinity. And that is as it should be, as we are divine ourselves, fragments of the godhead.

I should also clarify a bit. "Will" with a capital "W" is not identical with the will that we speak of in our daily, profane lives. Will is a divine emanation, which reaches expression within us. We often don't hear it clearly enough to be able to act in accordance with it.

SLACK: I'd like to know a little more about what time this is in the context of the witchcraft tradition that you practice.

PESCE: Okay. There has been a big rise in pagan practice, very much located at the heart of the technical community. When I was living in San Francisco the joke was, if you throw a rock you'd hit a witch. And it's absolutely true. There is something about the nature of the technology itself – I think it's acting like a mirror. And the mirror is very interesting. Cyberspace is a mirror that gets held up to the third eye. And the third eye, *ajna chakra*, is the light that removes illusion. It shows things as they are. And so this removal of boundaries, or refiguring of boundaries, that we're seeing is showing the world perhaps more clearly. I think we're in a powerful state of coming together. Through our own actions we can determine the form of that coming together. Is this going to become humanity as beehive, where the orders are delivered via pheromone, Internet, waveform, brain control, whatever, to a slave race where overall individuality has been lost? Or is this going to express itself in a kind of Cambrian explosion, a differentiation into a multivariate form, which understands its own internal organization?

Our own actions individually play in this. Can we change the overall stream of things? I don't know. There are limits to everyone's knowledge. I certainly don't claim any understanding of the future, other than that I do know that we need to work toward vivogenic ends in our own work as technologists. And that has been informed by my work as a witch. And witchcraft places very great care on the Earth, on the body of the planet as the great mother. That has definitely been a guiding light for me as I work.

SLACK: Does witchcraft emphasize the importance of biological diversity?

PESCE: There is no one particular form of the Goddess or God that is revered above anything else. This multiplicity of gods and goddesses is, I think, engendered by that same drive to diversity. And each form is particular. Each form has a domain and purposes, yet each is somehow descendant from an absolute form.

The practice of most of the creative people that I've had the opportunity to work with is eclectic and it's playful. Play may be the essence of what we see in the Cambrian explosion; nature is just playing in form. "Let's try this one, or this one, or this one." That also informs my own Craft practice and the Craft practice of others. I'm going to work magically with some people who are very highly placed in technology – and I won't give their names – to do a Samhain ritual, a ritual of Halloween. We are going to Death Valley. We have some guidelines, but we don't have anything hard and fast that we know we are going to do. There are specific forms that you do for a ritual period and you don't depart from those – they establish the space inside of yourself where you recognize the sacred immanence. But within that there is a lot of play and diversity. We're all bringing in our own elements to share in a sort of stone soup that represents, for us, what the religious essence of the event is about. I will learn enormously from everyone else's diversity.

I heard [psychologist and author] Sherry Turkle give a paper at a conference a few years ago where she expressed the ontological similarity between the users of multi-user domains (MUDs and MOOs) and people with multiple personality disorders. She suggested maybe this was the emergence of some new kind of self which could hold ideological distinctions and distinctions of ontology which we hadn't previously seen, or which had only been seen as pathological. There is a door there. And I think we are being forced – our children particularly, who are far more plastic at this than we are – to presume an ontological multiplicity, which may be a foundation for where we are going.

SLACK: I wonder if this is a movement away from being what is called "a whole person."

PESCE: It may very well represent a movement away from the Renaissance ideal of the singular, integral artistic ego. It may be a movement away from that, and it may be why I can, even in my own work, encompass as many contradictions as I do and not be disturbed by it. We just realize that we are contradictory, but that these contradictions produce at some level a greater harmony.

8 Mehdi Golshani

The Ladder to God

Mehdi Golshani is Distinguished Professor of Physics at Sharif University of Technology, Teheran, Iran, and is the founder and chairman of the Philosophy of Science Department of that University. He is also director of the Institute for Humanities and Cultural Studies in Teheran, Iran. He received his PhD in Physics from the University of California at Berkeley, and was a Senior Associate Member of the International Center for Theoretical Physics, Trieste, Italy (1990–1995). He was recipient of Iran University's Best Faculty Award (1992) and the John Templeton Science and Religion Course Program Award (1995). His research interests include particle physics, cosmology, foundations of quantum mechanics, philosophical aspects of physics, philosophy of science and theology. Among his recent books are: *The Holy Qur'an and the Sciences of Nature* (1997), *From Physics to Metaphysics* (1997) and *Can Science Dispense with Religion?* (1998, editor).

Golshani sees his science as one form of worship among others. The Qur'an directs us to study the works of God, he says, and science gives us tremendous tools to do that. And modern science provides much evidence for God's role in designing the universe. In particular, Golshani believes that the "fine tuning" of those physical laws and properties that make our universe possible at all, let alone hospitable to life, are strong evidence of intentional design. "The beauty of physics has shown us the existence of a mastermind behind things," he says.

But even though science is, in general, a very important ladder for understanding nature, it does not take us to the top. The methods and insights of science must be combined with those of metaphysics, philosophy and religious worship if the true nature of the world is to be known, Golshani says.

MEHDI GOLSHANI: I'm a Muslim by birth, and I started to study theology and philosophy when I was at high school. So, by the time I went to the university as a physics major, I had studied Islamic philosophy quite a bit. And that encouraged me especially to pursue physics. Well, I got my BS in physics from Teheran University, and then I went to the University of California at Berkeley where I got my PhD. That was during the 60s. Then I went back to Iran immediately and became associated with Sharif University of Technology, as a member of the Physics Department, where I have been since then.

PHILIP CLAYTON: So you were first interested in Islam and Islamic philosophy, and those interests led you toward the study of science? Did your advanced studies in science seem to be a natural extension of your practice as a Muslim, or was it sometimes difficult for you to see the connection?

GOLSHANI: It wasn't difficult at all. Many of the Muslim philosophers studied natural philosophy, philosophy of mathematics and metaphysics all at the same time. Of course the natural philosophy of the old time is gone. But that has not affected the theological or the metaphysical side, which I found to be consistent with the modern way of doing science. I considered philosophy and science to be complementary tools for understanding nature.

CLAYTON: How are your religious tradition and your science relevant to one another?

GOLSHANI: Science and religion are often seen these days as being either in conflict or independent. I see scientific work as one type of worship, alongside of others. We have been ordered to approach God in various ways. One way is to see His signs in the universe. The Qur'an is full of recommendations to see the signs of God in the universe and to discover the patterns of God in the world. That was the main motivating force for the early Muslim philosophers and scientists. The main incentive for their study of nature was to accomplish this Qur'anic assignment, that you have to think about the signs of God in the universe and discover its mysteries. So, nothing has changed my basic idea, even though I have gone through a lot of physics. I consider physics a sort of worship – nothing else.

Muslim philosophers and scientists saw the universe as a whole. When you read a book, you encounter different chapters. One is about physics, another is about cosmology and so on. The whole universe is like a book, which has harmony between its various chapters. This is the way they saw it. They didn't differentiate between various sciences and did not say: this is religion and that is science, et cetera. They saw all sciences as complementary, all being directed to a single purpose and all originating from the same metaphysics. In other words, science and religion were seen to share a common metaphysics. Here, I want to quote the Qur'an: "We belong to Allah and to Him we shall return" [2:156]. The Originator is God and the goal is God.

CLAYTON: In what respect, if any, has there been any change in this approach?

GOLSHANI: The general attitude has changed, especially after the Renaissance, and later through infiltration of Western ideas and Western science. So, while at the end of the first millennium, in the days of the Islamic philosopher and physician Avicenna, there was no separation between mathematics, physics and theology, later they became completely separated, and even now they are separate disciplines at our universities. A student at our universities, as in Western universities, learns science without paying attention to the philosophical or metaphysical implications of his discipline.

CLAYTON: Is this separation something that we should worry about?

GOLSHANI: I think it has been harmful. Even in the West, there have been a lot of changes in the last two decades. I see the revival of the same kind of thinking that was present in the Islamic civilizations. For example, the South African cosmologist George Ellis says that whereas we deal with regular cosmology with little "c," we have also to consider cosmology with capital "C," which has a larger perspective. This takes you to a higher dimension – a more perfect perspective of the universe. So, even in the West, there is a movement toward a more unified outlook.

CLAYTON: Could the movement also be a movement back to natural theology in the sense of the great Islamic thinkers who developed arguments from what they knew of the world towards God?

GOLSHANI: Natural theology, as we see it in some of the Western books, is different from the kind of natural theology that Muslim theologians developed. They considered science to be a prerequisite for understanding, but not as sufficient for it. It had to be supplemented by philosophical reasoning. Science is a ladder, but it doesn't take you to the top. It gets you up to a point, but, to go higher, you must add philosophical or metaphysical thinking. As I understand it, natural theology in the West is sometimes taken to mean that just by science alone, and nothing more, you can reach God.

CLAYTON: If I combine science with philosophy, could I build a ladder all the way to God?

GOLSHANI: I think so. But only if you do not consider philosophy in the limited sense, but admit into your philosophy that, besides the regular intellect, there are other ways of reaching God, and that there is a place for revelation. In other words, you must admit that there are other ways of getting to God besides science. In the Islamic philosophers' view, revelation had a special place. If philosophy includes or admits those channels, then combined with science, it could lead to God.

CLAYTON: But, ultimately, we would have knowledge of God only with His own self-revelation, right?

GOLSHANI: Yes, we get some knowledge about God through prophetic revelation and through our religious experience. But, in my view, there are certain things that you can get only through prophetic revelation. Thomas Aquinas said the same thing.

CLAYTON: In Islamic theology, what are the areas that bring your belief as a Muslim and your work as a scientist most closely together? Is it the common pursuit of truth in science and religion, or the nature of law as God built it into the universe in the beginning? What are some of the themes?

GOLSHANI: I think discovering the laws provides a tool, not an end by itself. God is the ultimate truth. So, discovering the laws of nature, or the patterns of God in the universe, are means, but not ends.

CLAYTON: Islam, like Christianity or Judaism, presupposes not only an arrow of time, but also a designed telos, an order to the universe. How do you see this classical notion of purpose in Islam fitting with contemporary physics?

GOLSHANI: There are two ways of explaining the harmony and order in nature. One, for example, is through Darwinian natural selection or chance, or by proposing many universes, ours being only one of them. I don't see these as satisfactory. I think the only explanation for the harmony and order in nature is the idea of a great Designer. Furthermore, I think that the great Designer had a purpose. So, in the Qur'an, we are frequently reminded that we are not created in vain. God says that we are created to worship Him, to get closer to Him and to be satisfied with Him. This is the main purpose of creation.

Since the Renaissance, Western scientists have left out this teleological idea. Scientists don't have anything to do with purpose in nature. They are busy with their discoveries and their predictions, et cetera. They don't necessarily deny that there might be a purpose, but they don't care about it. And some of them deny it altogether. For example, the Nobel Prize-winning physicist Steven Weinberg says that he doesn't see any purpose in the universe. But how does he justify his search of the unification of forces? Is it only a mental play? Is it only to have a super force? Well, what is the use of that? I don't see any explanation. If there is no purpose, then what is the use of his looking for the unification of forces? That's why after he wrote his book, *Dreams of a Final Theory*, another physicist, this one from Princeton, wrote that Weinberg was philosophizing in spite of himself: in his book, Weinberg was discrediting philosophy, but he himself was philosophizing at the same time. Einstein had a beautiful saying: "If you want to find out anything from the theoretical physicists about the methods they use, I advise you to stick closely to one principle: don't listen to their words, fix your attention on their deeds."

CLAYTON: You spoke before of a ladder and you said that science can take us only part of the way toward God. How much of

God's purpose can we discern within physics and astro-physics?

GOLSHANI: Consider the idea of fine tuning in the universe. You see a lot of fine tuning in the coupling constants of nature – the charge of the electron, the mass of the electron, the ratio of the various force constants of nature, et cetera. If they were different, the universe would be different, and it wouldn't be hospitable to sentient beings. This, I think, is a clear signal that something is going on there. Now, some people, in order to avoid a theistic interpretation of things, appeal to infinitely many universes, each with different constants. But they leave aside a much easier interpretation, which says that there is a Designer. When we see a sign we have to discern and be very thoughtful about it.

CLAYTON: Do you see recent work on the anthropic principle as further evidence of the special role of humans in the world?

GOLSHANI: The anthropic principle implies that we have a special universe that is hospitable to sentient beings. Some cosmologists attribute this fact to the existence of multiple universes. Others say a theistic interpretation is much simpler. Human beings are meant to be here, and they are here to fulfill a definite purpose. I think modern physics gives us clues, but we have to be insightful in our interpretations of these clues.

CLAYTON: Do you think there's an additional clue in the tendency of the universe to form more and more complex structures?

GOLSHANI: Yes, there we see hierarchies. This shows one possibility for preparing the ground for the emergence of life.

CLAYTON: Are there any other parts of the new physics that you could point to as evidence of this sort?

GOLSHANI: All of the new physics is full of mystery. We still can't explain the quantum world. We don't know anything about it. We don't even know what an electron is. Is it a wave? Is it a particle? We have learned from the new physics that the world is much more complex than some physicists thought. As physicist David Bohm says, there are hidden orders in nature. We shouldn't be content with the surface of science. We have to argue metaphysically, whereas we have been only content with mathematics and physics. Cosmology and the quantum physics have taught us about the immense mystery of the world.

CLAYTON: If the evidence had turned out to support Steady State theory instead of the Big Bang, would that be evidence against theism? Would that be bad news?

GOLSHANI: No, I don't think so. This is an old issue. Both Islamic philosophers and St Augustine said that in order for the universe to be created, it does not have to be created in time. I think it's a mistake to say that in order to have a theistic interpretation, you have to have a Big Bang at t=0. We could have a theistic interpretation for either the Steady State universe or for the Big Bang universe.

CLAYTON: Are there any imaginable results in physics that could falsify religion or that would be bad news for those who believe in God?

GOLSHANI: I don't think so. As far as a religious world view is concerned, we are ordered to discover nature through a journey. But sensory experience is not enough for this job. It has to be augmented by intellectual exercise and there is room also for inspiration. So, the job of science is left to the scientist. The holy books are not encyclopedias of science, though some natural phenomena are explained there. Those phenomena are just for illustration and to encourage us to seek the laws of nature. We are not entitled to be lazy and to try to read all of the laws of nature from the holy books. But we are taught some epistemological lessons, and we are also taught about some of the problems of the origin and the end of the universe. Otherwise, we are left free to find out about nature ourselves.

CLAYTON: In Islam, Christianity and Judaism, persons are specially created as free and morally responsible before God, to worship God, and to obey Him. How do you see this notion of person fitting with contemporary work in the sciences? Is there a conflict between the religious notion of a human being and the scientific one?

I wondered in particular what your reaction is to evolution, because it tends to make the human less unique and more like the other higher primates. Should religious persons worry about evolutionary theory?

GOLSHANI: No, I don't think that evolution, by itself, is against religion. It only says the creation of human beings as sentient beings is done through an evolutionary process. This doesn't make them unworthy. A scientist who emerges as a Nobel Prize winner is not the same person as the elementary school child he once was. But, the fact that he has gone through this channel doesn't diminish his value. If he had emerged as a PhD in physics at birth, that would not give him any more grandeur. It is the same with the evolution of species.

The moral and philosophical dimensions added to evolutionary theory gave it an atheistic interpretation for a lot of people. I think that even if you consider the human soul as a completely separate entity coming in at a later stage, you're not in conflict with the basic idea of evolution.

CLAYTON: Do Muslims believe that God could use the stages of evolution as a way to bring about his purpose?

GOLSHANI: Well, some scholars do and others resist that way of thinking.

CLAYTON: How do you tend to think about it?

GOLSHANI: In my view, evolution by itself, without the customary philosophical attachments of Darwinism, is not inconsistent with religion. At the same time, I think it is too early for a scientific verdict on this issue. We don't know enough about atoms or electrons, let alone complex systems like human beings. I think that even when we have learned about the electron, it still will be too early to say anything definite about the whole capacity of human beings. In any case, I believe that human beings have a dimension that differentiates them from the rest of God's creation.

CLAYTON: Even if God used the stages of evolution to bring about mankind, would God have to intervene at the end to specially create human beings with souls?

GOLSHANI: In Islamic philosophy and theology, God is engaged in the creation process at every instant. It's a continuing business. But it is implied in some of the Qur'anic verses that Man has an additional dimension that separates him from other things. But this would come after you reach a certain stage in the material domain. Then God adds an extra dimension. This is, in fact, what the well-known sixteenth- and seventeenth-century Muslim philosopher Mulla Sadra said. In his view, man starts as a material thing and at a certain stage, with the help of God, a supra-natural dimension is brought in.

Some contemporary scientists want to explain human soul on the basis of emergent properties in complex systems. They say that when you have a complex system, emergent properties appear. Now, what some Muslim philosophers say is that we go through this material ladder and then an extra dimension appears. But contemporary thinkers are thinking mostly on the materialistic plane. Mulla Sadra and his followers hold that soul is a supra-natural dimension. The consciousness, the spirit, or whatever you want to call it, is something different and comes after the material dimension.

The materialists think we can explain all things on the basis of physics or chemistry alone. Mulla Sadra held that there are other causes than material causes alone. We have two types of causes. We have transversal causes and we have longitudinal causes. The longitudinal causes include immaterial ones. In short, Muslim philosophers say human beings have an immaterial dimension that is different from what other animals posses.

CLAYTON: As long as philosophers were willing to say that a new, immaterial dimension arose, would that be adequate for Islam, or would there need to be direct activity of God to bring that about in the end?

GOLSHANI: Even other activities are not without God's intervention. But a special significance is given to man's spiritual aspect. In the Qur'an, God attributes the whole creation of man to himself, but there is an emphasis on his spiritual dimension: "Your Lord said to the angels: 'I am creating man from dry clay, from black moulded loam. When I have fashioned him and breathed of My spirit into him, kneel down and prostrate Yourselves before him'" [15 : 29–30].

Muslim philosophers believe that God acts through secondary causes. Even the immaterial dimension is brought up through secondary causes – through secondary *immaterial* causes. God intervenes in everything, but through secondary causes.

They believe in a longitudinal system of causes, where one could relate every occurrence to God as its source of existence. This emanation, however, takes place under certain terms and through certain means. These intermediary means are often called secondary causes.

CLAYTON: Are humans qualitatively different from any other animal in terms of, let's say, consciousness? And is that, for Islam, a unique characterizing feature?

GOLSHANI: Yes. I think that is a common view. Almost all of the philosophers that I know in the Islamic world think that way. They differ as far as the interpretation of evolution is concerned, but they all have this common view that human beings are different from other animals.

CLAYTON: Do you think there could be a science of consciousness? Or is that a theological matter from the start?

GOLSHANI: Well, I think we could improve our knowledge of consciousness, but I do not think that we can explain consciousness on the basis of experimental science alone.

CLAYTON: So we might have a science of law-like regularities in nature. We might have a science of evolution, but just as we would never have a science of divine purpose, so we'd never have a science of consciousness.

GOLSHANI: Yes, that's what I'm saying.

CLAYTON: So here's one area within the empirical world that could never be grasped by science at all.

GOLSHANI: Consciousness cannot be completely grasped by science. In the last two decades, some physicists, including some distinguished ones, have admitted that we may never be able to explain consciousness on the basis of physics alone. I share this view.

CLAYTON: So, this is important evidence for religious belief, that here we have a datum in the physical world, which is nonphysical and which can only be explained in theological terms.

GOLSHANI: Modern physics has been a good witness to the fact that we cannot explain a lot of things, even at the level of physics. We have not been able to explain, for example, the reduction of the wave packet so far, and we can't explain the origin of the universe at the moment. In fact, Godel's theorem disappoints us of getting a theory of everything.

CLAYTON: Let me ask you then about the traditional religious view of God as being present and active in the universe, creating humans, providing purpose and so forth. In general, do you see the traditional notion of God as having grown through recent physics, or remaining untouched by it, or has recent physics actually challenged the traditional beliefs about God in any way?

GOLSHANI: Well, it has both challenged and deepened our view. It has challenged it because some physicists and philosophers have tried to dispute arguments for the existence of God. For example, in the matter of the anthropic principle, they say that it can be explained on the basis of multiple universes.

But I think the discoveries of recent physics have also deepened our idea of God. Our ancestors were dealing with a very limited universe. But, now we are witnessing the immensity of the universe, and the fact that there are things that are behind the horizon that are not accessible to us because of the limitations for the signal velocity, et cetera. Therefore, the situation has changed in both a positive and negative sense. Previously, there were certain arguments for the existence of God. These arguments have been challenged in the last three centuries. But, the grandeur of our universe and its complexity have brought light for the believers.

CLAYTON: Now that we can predict the future more accurately and carefully in physics, some scientists claim that it's harder to attribute particular events in the world to God. With the growth of physical knowledge, for instance, is it harder to accept the idea of miracles?

GOLSHANI: No. First of all, I think those critics are mistaken in their interpretation of miracles. Miracles can be accomplished through both material causes and immaterial causes that are hidden from us. A hundred years ago, we could only see two forces in nature: electromagnetic and gravitational. Now, we are aware of four forces. In fact, we are explaining the main energy generation in stars in terms of the two recently discovered forces. There are so many things hidden in nature that we cannot deny that God could, through the intervention of those things, have brought something about without breaking the laws of nature. We cannot say that a miracle is the breaking of the laws of nature. It could be exactly according to the laws of nature, but those laws of nature that we are not yet aware of. The second thing is that causes are not confined to material ones. Thus, there is no conflict at all. Furthermore, with the advent of quantum mechanics and the development of chaos theory, the problem of predictability turned out to be more complex than physicists had thought.

CLAYTON: Would you say that miracles were compatible with a strong physical determinism if it turned out that the physical world was determined?

GOLSHANI: We believe that human beings have been given the freedom of choice by God himself. So, adding that dimension, I think there is no problem. We believe that natural laws are there and one of the items in the universe is this freedom of human beings. If you add this dimension, then you could explain other things. Some of the physicists of the early twenties, like Eddington, thought that the indeterminacy of quantum mechanics might solve the problem of human freedom. But to solve that problem, it is not necessary to appeal to quantum indeterminacy, as Einstein and others mentioned. Furthermore, a miracle takes advantage of some laws of nature that we are not aware of.

CLAYTON: Your own view sounds closer to that of the German philosopher, Kant, who said that the physical world could be fully determined, but there could be another world, the world of ends, of goals, in which humans live. In other words, we could be free in a totally determined universe. Is that an Islamic view?

GOLSHANI: We are part of the universe. We human beings, as free agents, are part of the universe. We are a factor to be reckoned with it.

CLAYTON: Some religious scientists in America have attempted to use quantum indeterminacy as an area where God could be acting in the physical universe without breaking any laws. Would you be sympathetic to such an idea?

GOLSHANI: No, I am not sympathetic to it at all. I think it is a God of the Gaps solution. They could only say that we have uncertainty in nature, because once we do an experiment, we interfere with the thing. So, it's only a matter of epistemological ignorance and not an ontological one. None of the things that physics has indicated so far suggests that we can abandon the principle of causality.

CLAYTON: Some religious scientists have said that we need to conceive of God more in transcendent terms and less in immanent terms, as we gain more physical knowledge. Is that a view that you would agree with?

GOLSHANI: I think transcendence is very important, but immanence shouldn't be forgotten either, and one should not replace one with the other. In fact, transcendence and immanence taken together express the proper relationship between God and the universe. Imam Ali elaborates on this point: "He is with everything but not in physical nearness. He is different from everything but not in physical separation."

CLAYTON: Is your general sense that the development of physics over the last few hundred years has given more opportunity for religious people to find the hand of God in the physical world?

GOLSHANI: Yes, I think the beauty of physics has shown us the existence of a mastermind behind things. Our world is not a trivial world. I think a religious person is in a much stronger position today than a few centuries ago. Compare our times with the era of the French mathematician and astronomer Laplace, who lived up to 1827. At that time, some scientists thought that they could explain the stability of the planets of our solar system without bringing God into the picture, and they thought that God was at most a watchmaker. Now we know that things are not that easy. The universe is evolving. It's dynamic. So, there is more room for the intervention of God at every instant – God is sustaining the world at every moment.

CLAYTON: Also, the role of consciousness – as observer effects in quantum mechanics, or in the anthropic principle, or in the study of the human beings – seems to be more central than it was for Newton, say.

GOLSHANI: Definitely, both with respect to the anthropic principle and also in the reduction of wave function of quantum mechanics, consciousness is thought to play a role. There is plenty of attention on consciousness besides just in the study of the brain. These extra factors, which came from physics, have given the study of consciousness a real boost. The large number of books that have appeared on the relation of physics and consciousness is a good witness to this assertion.

CLAYTON: Some religious thinkers have said that developments in physics and biology should be very encouraging to theists, but they have said it's more difficult for the specific, concrete beliefs that separate Judaism, Christianity and Islam. Do you see it that way?

GOLSHANI: Yes, I think the general belief in the usefulness of sciences for a theistic outlook has been deepened by scientific discoveries, but in all three religions the main trust is taken from the revelation.

CLAYTON: Are there results in science that are particularly encouraging for you as a Muslim compared to, say, a Jew, or a Christian?

GOLSHANI: No, I think explaining the universe in terms of one Almighty God, Who is omniscient and omnipotent, is common to all three religious. And the new discoveries of science have deepened that belief. As far as God and the transcendence of God are concerned, I don't see that much difference. Other scientists working in different environments might be thinking differently. I don't see that much difference when I discuss these ideas with my Christian or Jewish colleagues.

CLAYTON: Without taking away from the areas of overlap, are there any areas of science as a whole that you find particularly encouraging for Muslim belief?

GOLSHANI: I can't think of an instance of particular importance. For a Muslim, all creation is the work of God and all areas of science should strengthen his or her belief.

CLAYTON: Does religious inspiration guide or motivate you, personally, as a scientist?

GOLSHANI: Yes, religious inspiration is a very important and determining factor for me. I am presently involved with the foundational problems of quantum mechanics and cosmology, and some of my students are working in this exciting area. This area shows the mystery of the world more clearly, and the religious world view is an inspiring guide for me.

CLAYTON: Would you say that you have been inspired by the results that you and others have come to in your work in fundamental physics?

GOLSHANI: The more I have worked on physics, the more encouraging it has been for me. Physics reveals such wonderful aspects of our beautiful world. Yes, the inspiration has come from this, but I see a concordance between the outside world and the inside world, and I attribute both of them to the same agent.

CLAYTON: That's very nicely put. Do you think that the religious scientist has a special role for religious believers in his own tradition? Could the scientist, for instance, help encourage believers to study the empirical world in a more religious way?

GOLSHANI: Certainly, when they say that the whole thing is created with a definite measure, it means that the world is orderly and lawful. In fact, we are explicitly instructed in the Qur'an to go and find out about how the creation started. The Qur'an says: "Go in the earth and look around and find out how Allah started the creation" [29: 20].

I think a religious scientist could help the public appreciate science, and he could make use of it for religious training and understanding.

CLAYTON: And do you think that the scientist might also help the religious people in his tradition to be more open to evidence, perhaps less dogmatic?

GOLSHANI: Yes, I think so. As Pope John Paul II said, "Science can purify religion from error and superstition; religion can purify science from idolatry and false absolutes. Each can draw the other into a wider world in which both can flourish." But of course one has to be careful to avoid scientism.

CLAYTON: In Christianity, for example, believing scientists have helped pull some Christians away from what we call fundamentalism in this tradition, and to make them a little bit more open in their own beliefs. Do you think that the role of Muslim scientists could help bring the Islamic world to a different way of viewing its fundamental beliefs?

GOLSHANI: Well, this is a very delicate problem. And I don't think it is always approached in the right way, even in the Christian world. A scientist could be a religious person, but at the same time be under the spell of scientism. In that case, his giving instruction to a religious person could be damaging. But an insightful man, having enough metaphysical background, could help a religious person. As you have in the Christian world, we too, in the Islamic world, have both types of people.

CLAYTON: So the scientist who would do this well, would be very devout himself and very sensitive to the beliefs of the people, he might be able to encourage others in a gentle way to learn from his attitude of openness to the data.

GOLSHANI: Yes, I think so.

CLAYTON: The scientist could be a sort of model of contemporary religious belief, which is profound and deep and yet, at the same time, open and sensitive and humble in his claims.

GOLSHANI: Yes, if that scientist has a metaphysical background. But if he doesn't, that is, if he is interested only in mathematics and predictability and discovery, then my answer would be no.

CLAYTON: And have you seen some of this in the Islamic world, where scientists have played that sort of positive role?

GOLSHANI: Yes, I have.

CLAYTON: Are you optimistic that that role could continue over the next years?

GOLSHANI: Yes, I'm very optimistic, both for the Christian world and for the Islamic world.

9 Kenneth Kendler

Just, Loving and Random God

Kenneth Kendler is the Rachel Brown Banks Distinguished Professor of Psychiatry and Professor of Human Genetics at the Medical College of Virginia, and he is Director of the Virginia Institute for Psychiatric and Behavioral Genetics at Virginia Commonwealth University. He is also a clinical psychiatrist. He has published more than 300 articles and several book chapters and has received the Lieber Prize for outstanding research in schizophrenia as well as the Dean Award from the American College of Psychiatrists in recognition of his major contributions to the understanding of schizophrenic disorders. Much of his work focuses on the genetics of psychiatric and substance use disorders.

Kendler is a reform Jew who studies the Torah regularly and who also sits daily in the Buddhist practice of *zazen*. He often feels close to some kind of loving, kind and caring Supreme Being, an experience that contrasts sharply with the seemingly random and unjust suffering he so often sees in his work. How, he asks, can the idea of a just and compassionate God, so central to Judeo-Christian theology, be consistent with the absolute and brutal randomness of genetic mutation? "I see no justice in who gets childhood leukemia," he says. So how does Kendler reconcile these differing views of how and why things unfold as they do? "Wrenchingly," he says.

KENNETH KENDLER: My upbringing was culturally very Jewish but anti-religious. My parents come from that part of European Jewry who'd been for three generations, on all but one of my lineages, socialist and political and both anti-religious and anti-Zionist. They would have been working in the Polish labor movement, not in a Yeshiva. In late adolescence I was interested in religious issues in a general way. In high school, for example, I read William James's *Variety of Religious Experience*, and a fair amount about eastern religion, particularly Zen Buddhism. I didn't read a great deal about western religions, which I think was not atypical then. I grew up in Santa Barbara in the mid-1960s. In my second year of college I was flailing around a bit, trying to get some focus in my academic and personal goals, and I was offered the chance to go to Israel on a six-month field study. At the time, I felt the trip had three possible benefits: it would give me a chance to look back at my roots, it would allow me to leave school but not be eligible for the draft and it would really give me the distance I needed to think about where I was heading in life.

It was a seminal experience. I spent the first three months studying on a kibbutz and had a wonderful time. I got to know and came to deeply admire a number of the kibbutzniks there. I learned Hebrew relatively well and began studying the Bible. There were about twenty of us from the University of California at Santa Cruz. For the last three months of our time we were allowed to do anything that was vaguely structured. A number of people stayed on the kibbutz. Others scattered all around Israel. I decided to get more specific religious training and ended up at a Yeshiva designed for American and Canadian college-educated youth. The phrase in Hebrew is *Bal Tschvot*, meaning a person who's returning to the fold. I was fairly clear in my discussions with them that I was not seriously considering becoming an Orthodox Jew, but that I very deeply wanted to learn about that world. I had a quite intense experience for those three months, really living the life of the Yeshiva student.

My Hebrew was fairly good and I was able to achieve a reasonable mastery of the primary texts of both the Mishnah, which is in Hebrew, and the Tanach, the Hebrew Bible. The Talmud, which is written in Aramaic, was still a little hard for me. After I got back, I had the task of integrating that

experience. My relationship with my parents had been relatively easy much of my life, but now I was mad at them. I
remember confronting them; I felt they had provided me with
the outer trappings of a cultural identity without any of the
internal working parts. Orthodox Judaism was never very
viable for me, in part because of the strong upbringing I've
had in western scientific and intellectual pursuits. The
Orthodox framework is one in which you really need to
accept that the original Torah was given by God to Moses on
Mount Sinai and that all of the law that derives from that has
the same divine commandment. And although I can respect
that, it was clear to me that I couldn't personally accept it.

Reform Judaism, now my formal affiliation, is only
marginally satisfactory to me. In many ways it's watered-
down orthodoxy. So I have set myself on a trajectory which is
largely personal and scholarly. That is a reflection of my own
predilections. Since I left college, I have really made a serious
effort to study the Hebrew Bible. I have kept up my Hebrew,
and most Friday nights – family permitting, which is about
three out of four Fridays – I try to set aside several hours of
study. I have been slowly working my way through the books
of Genesis, Exodus, First and Second Samuel and most
recently Deuteronomy. I'm studying the Hebrew carefully and
studying a variety of commentaries. I've also been doing some
teaching at our synagogue. And I've been doing a fair amount
of studying in ancient Near Eastern religions. I've recently
been studying Mesopotamian mythology, particularly creation
stories. I do some, but less, work in the later Jewish traditions
of Mishnah and Talmud, in part because it's a little more
foreign territory to me, and that continues to be an important
part of my religious identity. My other religious strain is the
eastern religion connection. In college, before I went to Israel,
I spent a summer studying at the Zen Center in San Francisco,
a really high-quality institution, and since then I meditate on a
regular basis. I meditate every day I can, usually five or six
days a week. I meditate in the morning. It is partly an attempt
to focus myself on the fundamental aspects of each day, of
trying to appreciate each day as it comes, trying to collect
myself and prepare myself. But there is also a religious compo-

nent. It's interesting; when I got back from Israel I tried praying in a more traditional Jewish way. But for me the silence of *zazen* is a more profound form of prayer than a traditional Jewish Orthodox liturgy.

GORDY SLACK: Do you find that your religious study and practice influence what you study as a psychiatrist or how you go about studying it? And if so, do you see that as an asset or as a problem?

KENDLER: In large measure I have existed on a two-track approach. I do research and I pursue my religious thought and practice largely independently of one another. Now, there are fundamental ways in which that's not true and I'll try to comment, but I think that at sort of a workaday level that's how I've solved this problem. I'm not sure the solution is entirely satisfactory, but it does have a conceptual basis and it does stem partly from my being a psychiatrist. You can use different words for it. One set is "knowledge" versus "wisdom." The science that I pursue is on quite a different epistemological level than the religion I pursue, and the two don't use similar methods, don't have similar goals, and in some substantial way don't conform to one another. Maybe the best way to put it is to say that they complement one another. They really don't conflict, but they don't entirely exist on the same plane.

What is particularly critical for me is that we not conflate and confuse the two kinds of knowledge. This relates very much to my attempt to make sense of my identity as a psychiatrist, because part of what you do in clinical psychiatry is try to integrate the scientific knowledge we have about psychopharmacology and about neurotransmitters and brain function with the very human knowledge that you gain about people as you sit with them in a counseling or psychotherapeutic endeavor. I struggled in the early years with integrating the kind of human knowledge obtained by sitting in psychotherapy with patients and the knowledge you glean from the scientific literature. I had a patient in her mid-twenties who became depressed after a romantic break up. After eighty or a hundred hours of psychotherapy she and I became mutually convinced that her depression was strongly related to the death of her father when she was seven years old. She had never properly grieved, and the romantic interest she chose was older and resembled her father in some ways. The loss of that romance clearly echoed back and brought forth a series of very painful, self-derogatory memories and questions that she hadn't really very well resolved. I went to the research literature expecting to find empirical evidence that death in childhood predisposes adults to depression, and was surprised to find that there wasn't any. Later, I did a study of about two thousand women and was surprised to find that there's no statistical relationship. A parent dying early, statistically, does not predispose depression; whereas divorce and other marital problems in a family do. Here you have two sets of knowledge. You have the human knowledge that you acquired by sitting with the patient, that the death of her father contributed to her depression. You also have this large statistically sophisticated sample, careful methodological science, which doesn't support it. Could that be a model for religious knowledge and scientific knowledge? You can't disprove the psychotherapeutic insight by going to the scientific literature. They're just not the same kind of knowing. Part of what psychoanalysis represents is a real failure at differentiating those two kinds of knowledge. Psychoanalysis claims that the knowledge that we achieve in the setting of a personal contact, where you can note things with a great deal of certainty but no ability to test their validity, can really be conceptualized as a form of natural science.

SLACK: You have to flip back and forth between these two kinds of knowledge both within your clinical and research roles as a psychiatrist and as a scientist engaged in a spiritual quest.

KENDLER: Yes. On some level, my choice of psychiatry represents my struggle to compromise between my scientific goals and my religious goals. My statement that these exist entirely on two separate planes is not entirely true. Come to think of it, even as an undergraduate at Santa Cruz I majored in both biology and religious studies. It's not an accident that I've become a psychiatrist rather than a biochemist or a cancer geneticist. And it's been a bit of a devil's bargain for me; I research the nature of human nature. Why are we the way we are? What are the factors that make us depressed? How do we develop individual differences? How do parents relate to children in ways that influence their children's mental health? All of these, I think, are relatively fundamental questions about the human condition.

When I was a medical student at Stanford in 1974, the very first study I ever tried to do in psychiatry was to look at people who had severe forms of non-Hodgkin's lymphoma, who had on the average about four months to live. I wanted to examine the relationship between their religious beliefs and their coping strategies in their last months of life. But the oncologists refused to let me talk to their patients. Here we are more than twenty years later having recently published a paper looking at religiosity in a twin study that we're doing of mental illness. It looks at how familial factors influence religiosity, the dimensions of religiosity and the relationship between religiosity and vulnerability to various psychiatric diagnoses and substance abuses. Given the importance of religiosity in human behavior, it's appallingly poorly researched in the field of mental health.

SLACK: I guess psychiatry and religion have been seen by many as competitors for a long time. Maybe there's a built-in aversion.

KENDLER: Well, that's right. You can go back to the Freudian influence, of course, which is fundamentally anti-religious. There is still literature suggesting that religiosity is a bad thing for mental health. This is not what we've found. We found, for example, that internal religiosity – not so much the external form of being ritually compliant or ascribing to more fundamentalist Christian beliefs, but the internal sense of feeling a religious purpose or focus in your life and praying to God at times of stress – was a fairly good protector against the depressogenic effects of stressful life circumstances. That's very consistent with what I would have predicted overall.

So there are religious themes in my research; this two-track model has not been entirely the case.

SLACK: It sounds like you've made career choices that allow you to follow the ethical demands, or ethical suggestions, of your religious and spiritual life. Do you think that Judaism suggests ethical imperatives for researchers beyond scientific rigor? Are there moral ramifications of being a religious scientist?

KENDLER: I do. Judaism is very human-centered. I think the value of the human life plays a central role. I have just been studying the history of creation stories from the Sumerian, Babylonian and Assyrian traditions and seeing how they compare with the early accounts in Genesis. The striking difference is the man-centeredness. In the early Babylonian accounts, man is created as a slave for the gods, who tired of digging the canals and keeping the irrigation ditches going. That's not at all the account we have in Genesis chapters one and two, in which man is really the height of creation. There, God gives the world to man to have dominion over. So I think that part of that fundamental humanness and human orientation has played a role. There are ways in which I also see myself in the role of the Jewish scholar.

I'm not as good in more direct ethical ways as my wife is. She's a family practitioner and spends her time caring for people as a good doctor. I contribute to charities and try to do other things, but I don't join picket lines, and I don't demonstrate, and I'm not terribly socially active. I pursue an intensive research career of trying to seek knowledge. The Greek author Nikos Kazantzakis wrote, "What is God but the search for God?" That's more where my religious life has been. When I was at the Yeshiva, the Rabbi's comment was, "You'd make a great Rabbi, too bad we can't convert you in some way." I have that kind of pedantic mentality. And that's the part that I identify with very powerfully. And that is broadly part of the tradition, but I couldn't say that I see myself as being ethically driven. In the research work I do, my ability to help people is very remote.

SLACK: Going back for a second to the distinction you made between knowledge and wisdom, do you see those two objects of your study as having a single source, or do you see them as having different sources?

KENDLER: Certainly not a single source. Part of what you learn by studying the history of psychiatry is what terrible things that well-intentioned people can do to other people in the name of what they think is medicine; prior to the advent of scientific medicine we did terrible things to patients. From that I conclude that my ability to successfully judge the quality of the care that I'm providing is zero if not negative. I will always be able to convince myself that what I'm doing is helping, particularly in psychiatry because when we have variable outcomes we always attribute all the good things to what we've done, and all the bad things to the accidents of nature or the uncooperativeness of the patient. This leads me to be very hard-nosed about the scientific method. The only way we are going to advance this field is by applying the most rigorous kinds of conceptual perspectives. The field of mental health is completely Balkanized. There are people who work solely from the perspective of family dynamics, who think that everything is the result of geneagrams and cultural transmissions from grandparents. Then there are the social psychiatrists who think that everything is a result of poverty and oppression. And the biological psychiatrists who say everything is due to neurotransmitter abnormalities. All of them are ideologically driven. My identity within the field of psychiatry has been very much tied to saying, "Look guys, we have to treat human behavior the way we treat other things: scientifically. You may see it as bloodless – and I'm not saying I care for patients this way, because I don't – but I really need to take your hypotheses, get clear on the statistical methods you use to address the hypotheses, and that's the way we need to go." So that's what I mean by "knowledge." Knowledge is something that is ultimately testable, although there are times in the field of psychiatry when it's extremely hard to test and to replicate and still get what you mean across.

I think that human wisdom comes in many, many different varieties. I don't tend to like the Pollyanna-ish, Joseph Campbell "these-are-all-really-one-myth" view of things. I think human culture is very diverse, and in fact arrives at fundamentally different views, though there are some common connections across. Part of wisdom means facing the rather negative features of the human character; we're pretty aggressive. This is certainly something that as a Jew you have to face. The human capacity to see somebody who's not a member of your group as not human is frighteningly profound and has had tragic implications throughout our history. But it takes so little to see the other as someone not like you, someone who doesn't have your feelings, not like your friends, and therefore allows you to do all kinds of terrible things to them. That is part of our nature. We can deny it if we want, but history is clear on this point. So I think that we all find individual paths through. Certainly there are aspects for me of the wisdom of Judaism that I find very appealing, but some of it is very close-minded, some of it is very ethnocentric. But there's a tremendous amount of beauty in the tradition. And that has largely been my path.

However, the Zen path is also active. I read Tang Dynasty poetry and I've been reading some haiku and I read a little bit in Zen, but mostly what I do there is just meditate. I've done it long enough and read enough earlier in my life, that that's kind of self-perpetuating. But my thinking is more in this other Jewish tradition. But I certainly feel that there's not one way or one path. I think part of early phases of religious development in most cultures is to feel that you are the chosen people and your capital is the center of the universe.

SLACK: I have a feeling you misunderstood my question, though I'm glad you answered that one. I intended to ask about the source of that which you study. As a psychiatrist you study human behavior. As a student of religion you also study human behavior, its meaning and its history. You apply different methodologies in these two ways of studying human life. But I'm wondering if the object of study that these two methodologies are applied to is in any sense the same object.

KENDLER: Yes, I misunderstood your question. That's actually a more profound issue. My initial reaction is, I don't know. The kinds of things that I study on a routine basis are, How depressed are you? How much alcohol do you consume? Have you used cocaine? Do you hear voices? This is a level of human behavior that is fairly removed from the "How do I relate to God and view myself in the universe?" kinds of questions. Now of course, that's patently not true at points, because when I went to Ireland, half of the schizophrenic patients had delusions about being Jesus Christ or Mary. The religion was all over the place. I ticked a little box that was perched between grandiose or religious, but that was about all I did. I think ultimately the answer is yes, it has to be the same. Most of what we study is on a very concrete level: How does one function in life? Are you able to love successfully over long periods of time? Are you able to work in a meaningful fashion? Do you experience anything more than the normal level of sadness that we often will at regular events? I'm studying a more functional level of life. Religious adaptation is part of that whole. This is a new thought to me. I can't say that I feel very confident about just how to answer that question.

SLACK: It may be that there isn't a very straightforward way of answering it. Perhaps there's another way of approaching the same subject, though? What in your view are the remaining major questions in psychiatry and how do they compare to the big questions or the big mysteries in religion?

KENDLER: Oh my God! That's quite a question. How long do we have?

SLACK: You can throw out three questions, like prospective jurors.

KENDLER: Well it would be much easier to summarize what we do know in psychiatry, than what we don't know. I think that I could describe the current scientific issues very briefly. Important issues would include: what is the natural typology of psychiatric and substance abuse disorders? That is, are we dealing with very much man-made conventions, historically derived? Or are they real illnesses? Do they exist in nature in anything like the way we suppose they do? That's one question. We're only beginning to get an empirical base, rather than a preconceived basis, of the complex interplay between genetic and environmental risk factors for these disorders. And exactly how that kind of minuet will play itself out over time and the various disorders is just slowly emerging. Another question is: how will the rapidly advancing world of human molecular genetics interface with the world of psychiatry? That's something that we're right in the middle of. It is very unclear at this point, partly because we don't know in what form the genetic vulnerability of psychiatric disorders is coded.

I barely know where to start with the other part of the question. My religiosity has been very private. I putz around studying the Hebrew Bible and I've acquired some knowledge over time and read in some areas, but I'm not an academician in that area. It's a private journey for me, which is clearly connected with this period in history. This is a hard time to live in some ways. We're moving so fast. Families are torn asunder. My parents live in California, I live in the East. I'm scared sometimes of losing hold altogether of what I'm doing in this life. What Judaism represents for me is a powerful sense of continuity. When I sit down and study these texts, which not only my grandparents, but their grandparents and their grandparents before them back 2500 years, have studied and tried to make sense of, there is a powerful sense of belonging to something that is orienting. I'm frightened for my children in some sense. Nintendo and the computer and the TV. How will they center themselves? I don't think man was meant to live this way. We're meant to grow up in smaller communities with a much greater sense of continuity and structure.

I don't think I can tell you what I consider the large questions in religion. For me, it's a far more private endeavor of making sense out of my own life, out of the tradition within which I grew up, and trying to patch up what these last several generations did. Judaism was so rigid and doctrinaire and anti-intellectual that three generations in my family rejected it. I'm trying to sort of do a patch-job. And I'm seeing whether I can transmit it to my children. It's by no means clear how they're going to adopt it and whether this will succeed. It might die out in my generation. My kids might all intermarry. I think about that a lot and about how that would feel. I have a hard time relating to the second part of that question.

SLACK: Well, I think you did answer it.

You said that man was not meant to live this way, which raises another question. How do you reconcile the purposefulness of the Jewish God and the purposelessness of the post-Darwin universe? In some very fundamental ways they seem like deeply conflicting interpretations of the world.

KENDLER: "Wrenchingly" would be the quick answer. One way to see this issue is as the theodicy problem. If one believes in a God that has anything like the shape of Yahweh in his later permutations within the history of both Judaism and Christianity, part of that is clearly that there is sense in the world which He, or it, has imposed. It's hard to keep faith with that, even though I deeply want to. I am very much stuck astride those two. I read Harold Kushner's book *When Bad Things Happen to Good People*. I tend to be allergic to such titles, but it's actually rather profound. The simple idea that God is responsible for and willed certain things to happen is untenable to me; I see no justice in who gets childhood leukemia. No, it just wouldn't work for me for a minute. But does that mean that I don't try to think about events in my life as possibly being related to some broader sensible scheme? I clearly do. Are those two inconsistent? Yes, in some ways they are. And I don't really know how to cope with that difference. Kushner says that if you give me a choice between an omnipotent and omniscient God who allows these terrible things to happen and a God who is quite limited and is not responsible, I clearly would prefer the limited God. The other one is not sustainable to me. And I've had to endorse that. If there is some divine force in the universe, it is at a more basic level. A lot of what happens in this world is just bad chance. A cancer mutation has no consciousness, no good or evil. It just gets mutated or it doesn't, and it's just bad luck if you happen to inherit that. Or it's bad luck if your Dad's gonads got in the way of some cosmic x-ray coming through. There's no sense to it. But there are ways in which that's a profoundly un-Jewish thing to say. The book of Job tries to struggle with this. So I think I'm really stuck with these questions.

There are so many points in my life where I feel close to some kind of Supreme Being. It is consistently with a sense of the lovingness, kindliness, caringness of that Entity for both me as an individual and for the world and the species around us. Then I pick up a genetics journal and read through a report of the next terrible Mendelian disorder, and see that a single based pair substitution, from a C to a G in a single base pair, produces a mentally-retarded child whose fate is to die at age six and which represents a tortuous experience for whatever consciousness that child has, and certainly for his or her parents. I just get completely stuck. I cannot relate my understanding or emotional experience of God with this absolute happenstance. I realize that people with much more sophistication than I have dealt with this, but on a personal level I don't know how to relate my concept of deity, with the sense of His or Her concern for this universe, with random genetic mutation.

SLACK: I think that question bumps up against another one that must be central to the work that you do. Obviously human freedom is central to the teachings of Judaism, but as a psychiatrist you must see an awful lot of people who aren't acting out of free choice and whose predicaments are imposed on them. Even the choices that they do make in some sense aren't made freely.

KENDLER: Only the very naive think that we all begin life with a blank slate. No one who knows human beings well can believe that. We begin with a tremendous amount of individuality. It is as if a composer were given three major themes from which to compose a symphony. You can't change the themes, but you can change the way they interact with one another: how they start and how they end, and which one opens the symphony, and which is loud and which is soft. You can't go back to the beginning and change the way we are. I'm somewhat introverted and I can't change that. I have to live with it and I try to adapt and be positive and know my limitations. I try not to put myself into the two-hour cocktail party where I know I'll get anxious, bored and frustrated.

A lot of psychiatry is about helping people with their individual limitations and their vulnerability. You may be born with a vulnerability to alcohol abuse. And there is a fundamental unfairness in how this is distributed. At our university hospital where I worked as an attending psychiatrist fifteen years ago, most of the people coming in would be middle class and would have had a psychiatric disorder you could really treat. The case that I saw the day before yesterday is more typical now. This is a guy whose mother was a cocaine addict. He was a coke baby. His spare job in elementary school was to go sell cocaine to help raise money for the family. He started using cocaine when he was seven years old. He was in juvenile detention by the time he was twelve. It just went on and on and on. Now he's twenty-two. He tried to commit suicide. He didn't have a chance. That is just the distribution of both genetic and environmental variables for this individual. How could he have established a positive, psychologically healthy mode of life? It's just unfair.

SLACK: For a person like that patient, there is obviously still a role for individual choice.

KENDLER: That's correct.

SLACK: And it seems that Judaism and Christianity, too, accentuate the importance of that role. What do you think modern genetics, modern psychiatry and all that we're learning about the biological basis for human behavior, are doing to transform how we approach what's left over? As we become better at analyzing the environmental and genetic influences that form us, how much is left over for us to talk about and ponder?

KENDLER: I don't see that as so much of a problem. Modern man is not the first to discover that hereditary factors play an important role. I had a wonderful discussion with a seventy-five-year-old Irish widow who had had a fourth-grade education in the west of Ireland. She wanted to know in detail why we were interviewing her, and when we told her that we were trying to find out whether insanity ran in the family, she stood up, put her hands on her hips and laughed out loud. "Oh, doctor, anyone could tell you that."

These are not new ideas. We're investigating them in more rigorous ways. But the idea that human behavior is substantially shaped by these factors is not a problem. The nugget of the issue is: does that really impact on the ethical consequences of making decisions? I don't think so.

People do make critical choices. They're not working from the same substrate; again I use alcohol as an example. It was no great ethical shakes for me not to become an alcoholic because for me one drink's fine, but I don't feel good after two drinks and after three I just feel awful. For other people it's a much more difficult decision. It's both much more pleasurable for them to drink and they may suffer fewer immediate consequences. It's the same with nicotine. But do I feel that because some individuals have higher levels of aggression than others, that that makes our ability to assign ethical responsibility for assault or murder more difficult? I don't have much of a problem there. We have predispositions, but that's not the same thing as making them part of the conscious decisions that we make. It's not a blank slate, but it's not mandated either. Genetic factors operate in a very probabilistic way. There are not genes that make you smart or genes that make you alcoholic, though there are genes that may incline you toward these. But they weigh in with a whole constellation of other factors.

SLACK: Those other factors may not be genetic, but science may reveal that they may be in some other sense deterministic.

KENDLER: Well, probably. But you know, we studied trying to predict people's history of depression. We studied every damned thing we could think of, including genetic background. And we ended up predicting 50 percent of the variants. And that's very good for human behavior. We thought it was tremendous. Psychology is just not at the point where we can even conceive of predicting 80 or 90 percent of why people are depressed. Humans are inherently so complicated and unpredictable. Maybe at some point this will be an issue, but right now it's hard for me believe that it will be pressing anytime soon, at least for these broad behavioral things we're talking about. That's not true for things like cystic fibrosis, where gene effects exist at a very much more direct level. For whatever reason, personally, this has not been such a pressing issue for me.

Also I've made an effort to avoid getting involved in legal situations where this might come up. So if a lawyer calls me and says, "This defendant's father was schizophrenic, and now we want to defend him on the basis that he has a genetic vulnerability," I don't want to get involved. Maybe I have a personal aversion to this as the key issue.

SLACK: When you look back on the history of your career, do you see any link between points of discovery in your life as a scientist, as a psychiatrist, and moments of religious insight or religious discovery? If your scientific and religious lives are lived in parallel – which I realize you haven't quite said – are those lives communicating?

KENDLER: Only modestly. This project I told you about is one such very faltering first step of trying to set up a cross-link between them. Clinical psychiatry is more connected, partly because that is so whole-human. One cannot, at least I can't, as a human being with some sensitivity, go through clinical training in psychiatry and not be profoundly moved by the experiences that you share with people. So that is more religious with a lower case "r," in terms of the depth of human experiences. Unfortunately in this end of the business they're often much more painful than they are beneficent. I would say that the intellectual work and the clinical work roll largely on separate tracks.

SLACK: Has anyone conducted the study that you originally wanted to do, back in the 1970s, looking at the relationship between religiosity and coping with impending death?

KENDLER: Not to my knowledge. I can't imagine why someone hasn't, but I don't know of any such study.

SLACK: Maybe as your Irish subject says, anyone who knows people who've died will be able to tell you that there's a relationship between religious faith and the ability to cope with death.

KENDLER: I expect so.

10 Joel Primack
Transcendental Theory

Physicist Joel Primack is best known for his fundamental contributions to cosmology, especially the theory of Cold Dark Matter and its recent variants. Cold Dark Matter remains the vanguard theory explaining the formation and distribution of galaxies and other large-scale structures in the universe. Primack has also forged new tools for exploring cosmological theories by employing some of the world's largest supercomputers to run various cosmological scenarios. He is also known for his work in particle physics, such as his early prediction of the mass of the subatomic particle known as the charm quark. Primack is a Fellow of both the American Physical Society and the American Association for the Advancement of Science. He earned his PhD in particle physics from Stanford University in 1970.

Primack holds that a people's confident understanding of their place in the cosmos is essential to their spiritual identity. Calling this a "golden age" for cosmology, he expects the new data pouring in from the Hubble Space Telescope and other new instruments to go far in helping establish the first verifiable theory of the history, structure and destiny of the universe. In addition to his research, Primack and his wife and collaborator, Nancy Abrams, teach a course on Cosmology and Culture at Santa Cruz, where he is a professor of physics. For several years they have been exploring ancient cosmologies – including that of the Kabbalah, the Jewish mystical tradition – and their relationships to modern cosmological theory.

JOEL PRIMACK: I am Jewish. My parents were both brought up in

Orthodox families, and for the first few years of my life, when my maternal grandmother was living with the family, we still kept kosher. I spoke Yiddish with my grandmother until she died when I was about three and a half. From when I was age six to age thirteen, my family lived in Butte, Montana, where, when we first arrived, there was one rabbi. He was a nice young fellow who taught me some Hebrew and Jewish history, but he left after a few years. When it came time for me to study for my Bar Mitzvah, the only rabbi in Montana was 200 miles away, in Billings.

PHILIP CLAYTON: Your family was Conservative at that time?

PRIMACK: No, Reform. But the distinction was pretty moot given that there wasn't even one regular synagogue in town. There was a minyan, a group of ten or more Jewish men, and occasionally my father participated. And I think that they used to bring in rabbinical students for Rosh Hashanah and Yom Kippur. We had many services at people's houses. But the established congregation in Montana was in Billings, and I had an aunt and uncle who lived there. So, starting at age ten or eleven, I used to make regular trips to Billings. I felt special; I used to ride the Northern Pacific all by myself, riding in the big domed Vista Cruiser through the Rockies. I would get out of school around noon on Friday and get to Billings in time for the Shabbat dinner at six or so. I'd work with the rabbi on Saturday and take the train back home on Sunday. For a couple of years I did this every other week or so, and then, as it came closer to my Bar Mitzvah, nearly every week. I had more or less a Conservative Bar Mitzvah. There was a lot of Hebrew, both the Torah for that week and also several Haftore portions. I remember that the Haftore included the famous lines from Isaiah about beating swords into plowshares. The talk that I gave in my Bar Mitzvah was about science and religion. My daughter read it when she was preparing for her own Bat Mitzvah several years ago. So did my wife and I. We were amused at how some of the themes that were in that talk are still themes that I think about today: basically, that there's no necessary conflict between science and religion, and that each can illuminate the other.

CLAYTON: What happened to that confident Bar Mitzvah assertion as you began more advanced studies in science? Did it get
repressed at all?

PRIMACK: Not really. I never saw any obvious conflict. Partly of
course, that's because the version of Judaism that I know is
not dogmatic, except of course that Jews are sure there is only
one God.

CLAYTON: Can I ask whether through the years you've done any
reading in the Jewish philosophical tradition and if it has been
an influence in your thinking and practice?

PRIMACK: I think even before my Bar Mitzvah and certainly afterward, I've been every so often fascinated by one or another
topic in Jewish thinking, literature, history, whatever, and I've
read a great deal. I should probably back up and say that
when I was not more than eight or nine, I had already read
the essays in Einstein's *Out of My Later Years*.

CLAYTON: So that's where the Bar Mitzvah talk came from?

PRIMACK: In part, probably, although I was a tremendous reader.
I had moved from California to Montana, and never got used
to the weather in Montana. I stayed indoors more than most
of my contemporaries. I used to easily devour ten books a
week. There was a wonderful little library in Butte and I read
all through the children's section. By the time I was nine, I had
special permission to use the adult section and I had read
every article in *Scientific American* from when it became a
modern magazine in 1947 up until the mid-fifties. In addition
I read a lot of philosophical stuff and Jewish literature and so
on. But I was very much influenced by Einstein, including of
course his essays on science and religion.

To the extent that I consider religion in my scientific
thinking, it's more or less in the Einsteinian way: that there is
no personal God, but that there is definitely a religious aspect
to the orderliness of nature – something that humans can
uncover with enough work and insight.

CLAYTON: Is that something we actually have scientific evidence
for? Or is it a religious claim?

PRIMACK: I think it's religious. But to be sure, there is evidence for
it. Scientists in general, and theoretical physicists in particular,
are basically idealists: Platonists, to some extent. We believe

that deep down the world is mathematical, not just described by mathematics, but inherently mathematical. And the laws are basically mathematical. So in some sense, God is mathematical. But there is no amount of evidence that can really prove such a thing. This is more or less an article of faith.

And the philosophically inclined physicists I've talked to about these things tend to share these views. Moreover, this sort of religious viewpoint, which of course can be expanded into just a sort of general belief in the success of the scientific approach, or the approach that physicists follow, is something that is confirmed by religious experiences.

I have, on several occasions, had the great good fortune of working out some theoretical idea and subsequently finding out that the world matches it. In other words, I've made predictions that turned out to be true, or close to true. It's an amazing thing to have just in your mind apprehended something possibly fundamental about how the world works, and years later discover that that's how it really is. It really does have the flavor of a religious experience. You wake up in the middle of the night in a cold sweat. You have to pinch yourself to confirm that it's really happening. It raises goose bumps. It gives you a feeling of being very close to the way it all really is. Sometimes, when you do a calculation or you follow through a chain of thought, you have this wonderful feeling that, ah, this is really quite beautiful, and it's neat and so on. That's one kind of feeling. But that's not the same as knowing that it is also true.

One of the first times that this happened in my own scientific career was in 1972. Together with two other physicists I calculated the mass of the charm quark. At that time nobody knew that charm was even right, and in fact I was pretty much persuaded that it was wrong. For one thing, our calculations concluded that it would be between one and two times the mass of the proton. That energy range had been pretty thoroughly explored, so I was pretty sure such things couldn't exist. And I had a prejudice that the whole charm idea – that there was an extra quark, a fourth quark – was ugly. But in 1974, the first particles that had charm quarks in them were produced at the SLAC Collider and at Brookhaven National Laboratory. I was here at Santa Cruz, but I got a call and was told, "Come up to SLAC; there's going to be a very important announcement that will concern you." So I was there for the announcement, and of course both the people who made the announcement got the Nobel Prize a few years later. Until the discovery, I was pretty sure that the charm idea wasn't interesting, that it was wrong. In fact, part of the reason it was given the name charm was to ward off the bad feelings that would be associated with such an ugly idea. Because of my prejudice against charm, I dropped the subject and worked on other things – and thereby missed out on an important opportunity. This taught me humility: don't presume to know more than the data permits; if several possibilities appear plausible, work all of them out. On the other hand, my calculations were right on: the charm quark is about one-and-a-half times the mass of the proton. By the way, from our modern perspective, charm looks rather pretty.

CLAYTON: It sounds like there are two different things you are calling religious here. The first is that the world really is mathematical, and therefore that you can move with confidence through it given what mathematics predicts.

PRIMACK: Yes, and the second kind comes only after the data are in, when it turns out that the calculations agreed with the observations. Other physicists that I've compared notes with have had this experience of predicting something on the basis of hypotheses that were by no means certain. When it turns out that your prediction is really true, that's eerie.

CLAYTON: Is it analogous to what it must have been like to Moses, who suddenly saw this burning bush and heard the voice of Reality itself?

PRIMACK: Maybe Moses heard a symphony and I heard just one note, but it's a little bit like a voice from Reality itself. For weeks or months afterward, this sort of eerie feeling would come to me. Einstein also liked to talk about how God told him this or that, or God doesn't play dice. There is a certain sense of contact with the way that nature really is underneath it all that one gets after a certain amount of success doing physics. It certainly bears some relationship to religious, even somewhat mystical, experiences.

CLAYTON: The mystical experience where God reveals himself in some way to a person? Is it that revelatory moment that's analogous?

PRIMACK: Yes, except the moment often occurs when you're doing the calculation, and the revelatory aspect is only apparent later on. I mean you sort of hope for it when you're doing it, but you're never sure, especially when you're working on the frontiers. You don't know if the input assumptions have anything to do with the world.

CLAYTON: A religious experience with a time delay built in?

PRIMACK: Yes, although— It's different from other kinds of religious experiences. But there is something religious about it. For one, it confirms these beliefs that tend to drive scientists to do the work that they do.

Most scientific work is routine. But one paper that I wrote with Sandra Faber, George Blumenthal and Martin Rees was kind of a capstone to a series of papers I'd written earlier. This was published in *Nature* in 1984, and it put forward the fairly developed set of ideas that's called Cold Dark Matter. That paper is now regarded as a classic. The theory that was presented in there correctly predicted the cosmic background radiation anisotropies, the difference in temperature in different directions, essentially as the Cosmic Background Explorer (COBE) satellite found. On April 27, 1992, the COBE team basically announced that they had discovered what our theory had predicted in 1984. That was quite an experience; in some ways more powerful than the 1974 experience, because this was much more daring. Our theory assumed things about the origin of the universe and the nature of the dark matter, neither of which are really known to be true even now. But the theory gave a very nice account of all the available data on the distribution and properties of galaxies. And this was the first time that anybody had had such an overarching theory that had a chance to do all those things. And of course it had a big impact on the field. Most cosmologists, especially observational people, tended to disbelieve theories, because theories were a dime a dozen and there was very little data. But Cold Dark Matter is certainly a theory that was taken much more seriously because it was very predictive. If wrong, it should have been easy to rule out, but it kept being more or less confirmed.

The basic idea that I'm trying to get across is that from the early eighties up until 1992, when the COBE discovery was announced, we had no idea that any of our input assumptions were right. We were pretty sure that there was such a thing as dark matter, although not a hundred per cent sure. We still don't know the nature of the dark matter, we don't know whether cosmic inflation is right, and these are two of the ingredients in the Cold Dark Matter theory. We didn't even know that there were primordial fluctuations, slight differences in the density from place to place that would give rise to galaxies. That assumption has been confirmed by COBE, and we now have a great deal of confidence that the general approach pioneered in our early work is right.

I sort of lived in an imaginary universe for many years. As a scientist I'm always aware it is just imaginary. But when it turns out that this imaginary universe that one has constructed actually bears some profound relationship to the real thing, there's something absolutely wonderful about it; and it has been an inspiration that has kept me going through years when things didn't seem to work. So, I've drawn inspiration – and I think it's even, in a certain sense, a religious inspiration – from scientific success. Some people would not be comfortable calling this religious, but I am.

CLAYTON: You use the word "religious" fairly easily. You use it in a very broad sense, one that Einstein and many others would have understood. How about connections with your religious practice more specifically as a Jew?

PRIMACK: For many years, whenever I encountered a religious person who seemed particularly insightful, one of my standard questions was, what difference does it make to your religious views that we live in an expanding universe? In the early 1990s, I went to one of Michael Lerner's salons in Berkeley. Lerner had started the magazine *Tikkun* a year or two earlier and he lived just a couple doors down the street from some old friends that my wife and I sometimes stayed with. Michael asked me if I'd read Gershom Scholem's book on Kabbalah, *Major Trends in Jewish Mysticism*. I'd read the first few chapters, but he said that I hadn't gone far enough. He told me to look up *Tzimtzum* and keep going. So I did. Then I read a number of additional things by Scholem and other books on Jewish mysticism. I was struck, as anybody is struck who studies this stuff, by the similarity between the basic picture of the origin of the universe in Kabbalistic stories and our modern conception. And it's more than just the basic idea of expansion or contraction of God – *Tzimtzum*. The first few *Sephirot* [the ten Kabbalistic aspects of God's emanation into this world] also have a remarkable correspondence with some of the ideas connected with inflation and eternal inflation, which may have preceded the Big Bang.

Kabbalistic thinking regards the first three of the *Sephirot* as cosmological. The first *Sephirah*, *Keter*, or crown, resembles the beyond-all-human-comprehension idea of God, the Maimonides sort of God that can only be approached in a negative sense: not finite, not anything that you can conceive of clearly. The next of the *Sephirot* is *Hokhmah* and the third is *Binah*. Both can be translated as wisdom. *Hokhmah* is the breaking through, the spark of understanding, the flash that contains everything. *Binah* is more like the understanding a mother has of her child, an understanding that grows. *Binah* is the becoming. If the ending of cosmic inflation and the beginning of the Big Bang is identified with *Hokhmah*, and the subsequent evolution of the universe with *Binah*, then eternal inflation, the creation of the many universes, quite naturally becomes identified with *Keter*. It's at the edge of human comprehension.

Of course, the danger in any of these identifications is idolatry. But the neat trick of the Kabbalists is to say that all these ten emanations of God are not God. God is beyond all of it: *Ein Sof*, the Infinite. So *Keter* is the closest you can come, but you're still not there. That sure sounds an awful lot like the Big Bang to me, like the creation event itself and the very, very rapid changes that must have occurred as the universe cooled and the symmetries broke and so forth.

CLAYTON: How would you explain that parallel?

PRIMACK: I don't have any particularly clever explanations, so I don't attempt to explain it. I don't even think we know where the Kabbalists got it. The basic idea of the *Sephirot* is in the oldest of the Kabbalistic books, called *Sefer Yetzirah* [Book of Creation], which is variously dated from the second to the sixth century CE and probably was written by Jews in Palestine. But the ideas bear some resemblance to ancient Pythagorean and Egyptian mythology.

CLAYTON: What do you make of the juxtaposition of the ancient cosmogonies and contemporary cosmology?

PRIMACK: The part that I find interesting is where you go after you see that there is a similarity. Although I don't know why those ancient ideas are similar to our modern scientific models, the Kabbalists used them in complicated, interesting ways in their culture. It was important to them. Maybe we can learn something from them about how to make sense of modern cosmology.

CLAYTON: Let me jump ahead here. Judaism, like Christianity and Islam, holds deeply embodied beliefs about the purpose and destiny of the created universe. It's crucial to that belief to presuppose not only an arrow of time, but also a designed purpose or end. In your view, how does the classical notion of purpose fit with perspectives shaped by contemporary physics and cosmology?

PRIMACK: Well, it's certainly true in the ancient Hebrew conception. There is definitely a direction of time. The world is, if you like, the unfolding of God's will. And fortunately, I suppose, for a scientist who also was raised in this tradition, there's obvious consonance, at least in broad outlines, between what we know scientifically and the perspective that the world is a process going only in one direction. I think it was Pope Pius back in the early 1950s who declared that it was great that it looks like the Big Bang is right. I can sympathize with that. It would have been tougher on us Judeo-Christians if it had turned out otherwise.

CLAYTON: "Tougher" on? There are people who would call it a "falsification of." Is that language too strong for you?

PRIMACK: I think so. I don't read the Bible literally. I'm convinced by the analyses of the Bible that take it apart and, for example, see at least four main texts in the Torah. If you study it, this just leaps out at you. The Hebrew Bible certainly arose out of a matrix of Middle Eastern religious ideas, though with a big twist: monotheism.

CLAYTON: So it can't be read literally, because it's a compilation of various textual traditions brought together over time? Is the complexity of the cultural genesis enough to make any talk of an empirical falsification of, say, Jewish belief, inappropriate?

PRIMACK: I think so. Again, I'm not a fundamentalist. I read the Bible as a kind of elaborate metaphor system, a mix of mythology, legends and real history. I don't need to worry about falsification in the scientific sense; it's not scientific literature.

CLAYTON: Yet, a few minutes ago, you said the Big Bang was good news for theists.

PRIMACK: Yes, well, for theists of this particular stripe. It might not be such good news for Hindus, who have a cyclical picture of reality. The Christian and Jewish viewpoint is comfortable with the basic linear evolution of the universe. On the other hand, there are elements of discomfort. The creationists read *Genesis* to imply that the animals that exist today are exactly the same animals that were created by God. I suppose it could be read that way, though it seems unnecessary. All of the ancient Middle Eastern traditions – the Egyptian, the Sumerian, the Babylonian, certainly the Hebrew tradition – present a flat-earth picture. The waters above were separated by the firmament from the waters below, it says in *Genesis*, basically to create a little space for an earth that we can live on. This bears no relationship whatever to our modern picture of what the universe really looks like. So the sort of attempt that Gerald Schroeder made in his book *Genesis and the Big Bang*, to try to see any kind of simple parallel between the *Genesis* story and our modern story, is doubly wrong. It not only does terrible violence to our scientific ideas, but also to the religious ideas that are expressed in the Bible.

CLAYTON: So there's also a loss to the religious power of the text when it's pushed on to this Procrustean bed of modern scientific theory?

PRIMACK: Yes. The text after all contains great poetry. And there is coherence to each of the different parts. It bears very careful study. But I don't think it's useful to ignore the context, and try to, as you say, force it into the Procrustean bed. I have no sympathy with that at all.

CLAYTON: Would you allow me to push you a little bit on your use of the word "compatibility"? Could there ever be anything stronger than compatibility? Would empirical confirmation of the texts be a category mistake, just like empirical falsification?

PRIMACK: Yes, except for the explicitly historical chronicles. It would be a category mistake. The word "consonance" would be much better. I think of the religious texts as being more like literature. There certainly can be similarity in the approach or style between the art of a certain period, or of a certain artist for that matter, and other ideas of the time. In the same sense, I think that there can be consonance, that is a good word, or complementarity, between certain religious ideas and scientific ones. The basic arrow of time of Judaism is like that. On the other hand, there's very little in Judaism, certainly not in the Judaism of the Torah, pre-Babylonian-exile Judaism, concerned with where this is all heading. There's the covenant and Abraham was promised that his people will be a multitude and that they'll play a special role in the world.

CLAYTON: But the messiah is missing, and even eternal existence of the soul seems—

PRIMACK: Exactly. There is none of that. In fact, there's no discussion of afterlife whatever. And certainly it's plausible to read that omission as a reaction against the ancient Egyptian preoccupation with those topics. That kind of Judaism actually appeals to me very much.

CLAYTON: Pre-Babylonian-exile Judaism?

PRIMACK: Right. In the Babylonian exile, the Jews came in contact with the Babylonian calendar, but also Zoroastrianism, and a strong sense of good versus evil. And the later Biblical literature begins to have a fair amount of that. It is also concerned with afterlife.

CLAYTON: The Hebrew Bible is famous for a lack of metaphysical interest. Even obedience to Yahweh is more an ethical injunction. One doesn't speculate about the nature of the divine.

PRIMACK: Exactly. I like that. I've never found the excessive theologizing of Christianity to be comfortable.

CLAYTON: And it's radically ethical. The obedience of Yahweh's people, of the people of Israel was of overriding importance.

PRIMACK: Absolutely. The sort of Judaism that I learned as a kid emphasizes duty. Proper behavior, including observance, would be far more important than any kind of belief. I participate in Jewish rituals without any great sense of belief in anything, although I often find the words very interesting, especially the references to the universe manifesting the greatness of God. This is just the way I was brought up and I enjoy it.

The fact is, my life and work are religiously motivated, in the sort of Einsteinian religious sense. But it's deep. It is not something that I take lightly. And I am a person with a considerable sense of duty, which has led me to help create new institutions such as the Congressional Science Fellowship Program, for example. I also have at one time or other devoted considerable effort to energy policy, arms control and other public issues. I'm sure that has to do with the way that I was brought up. Actually, Einstein says that for an advanced religious thinker morality has nothing to do with belief in any kind of God. Morality is just something that's taught to all children in a well-organized and well-functioning society. I'm not sure that that's a really satisfying approach for most people. It seems to be okay for me. Of course, to be taught convincingly, morality needs to be modeled.

I don't label myself as agnostic, and certainly not as an atheist. An atheist basically is just looking for a fight. But most of the time I don't even think about whether there is a personal God. Occasionally, when I've been under severe personal stress, I've prayed in a very serious sense. So I understand when other people do it. I don't know whether it is wishful thinking or not, but it has worked for me. So I certainly understand that it works for people at various times. But rationally, I have a hard time taking seriously the idea of the standard omnipotent, omniscient God, who intervenes and cares about human affairs. For all kinds of reasons, including the limitations imposed by the speed of light, that doesn't make a lot of sense. On the other hand, I occasionally am comforted by that feeling, as I think many people are. And later on, when I look back on it, I think, well it was probably wishful thinking. On the other hand, I do believe that the universe is orderly, beautiful and in some deep sense good, and also that, remarkably enough, it's something that humans can understand.

CLAYTON: Would you say that the universe seems to have a sort of purposefulness?

PRIMACK: Freeman Dyson wrote in one of his essays that the universe seems to have been designed for life, even for life of our type. Others have written about what's sometimes called anthropic cosmology. There's no question that the universe does seem exquisitely designed for critters like us. If it were different in any of numerous ways, it would be a lot less interesting. For one thing, we wouldn't be here. What's not clear, is whether that means that some intelligent creator created it with us in mind. That certainly is a simple explanation that fits the facts. But so do other scenarios. Maybe there were zillions of universes created and we just happened to live in this one. Of course we couldn't have lived in any of the others, because they wouldn't have been appropriate for creatures like us.

The trouble with the intelligent creator idea is that it's scientifically sterile. It stops you from asking the right scientific questions. The question that really interested Einstein was whether God had any choice in the creation of the universe. That's remained one of the most important questions for physics to confront. It's a very tough one, and we may not have the necessary tools to address it yet. But we'd like to know what the range of possibilities is. And to say that it was all created by an intelligent creator with a plan in mind suggests that there were many different possibilities. Physicists want to discover a set of physical laws that could result in only one possible universe, where there wasn't any room for a creator to make choices.

The safest thing to do as a scientist is to be agnostic on that issue, to leave open the possibility that there was no choice, that there's only one kind of universe that's possible. Eventually we may make enough progress so that we can start to address Einstein's question.

CLAYTON: Wouldn't it be even better news for science if not only was only one universe possible, but if it had to come into existence on its own, according to some sort of metaphysical laws, rather than needing the agency of a supernatural being?

PRIMACK: It would be a success for physics if we could also figure out the nature of the initial conditions as they followed from some set of physical principles. Certainly that's the approach that we're trying to follow. In this general scheme that involves cosmic inflation, what we're trying to do is to figure out why the initial conditions of the Big Bang were the way they were. There are alternative approaches. Stephen Hawking, for example, suggests that if you go back far enough in time you just start coming forward in time again. In that model, there isn't any edge that represents the beginning of time. The religious implication of Hawking's view, of avoiding a creation event, is not clear to me. But the practical problem here is that we just don't know how to test these theories. Inflation hides whatever came before it. And we're talking about a situation where both quantum mechanics and gravity are important. In the next few years, we may know enough about quantum gravity to get somewhere.

CLAYTON: Judaism, like Christianity, views God as present and active in the universe, giving human freedom and arranging things. Is the kind of God physics should assume bad news for Judaism?

PRIMACK: As a physicist I'm better off not assuming the presence of an active God and leaving that question open for investigation. If you mean miracles – that is, violations of the laws of physics – then I don't believe in them. I've never seen any evidence for them, and if the laws of physics even have one violation, then they're wrong. And they're not wrong, so I don't believe in miracles. On the other hand, if in a sort of Spinoza-type way you identify God with the universe, as the organizing principle of the universe, or the forms behind the apparent, then there's certainly order in the universe; and it's an order that's deeper than we yet understand. It makes sense to identify that with God I suppose, certainly some people do and I have no problem with that.

CLAYTON: Especially given the religious nature of thinking about that order, and discovering it empirically.

PRIMACK: Exactly.

CLAYTON: But providence?

PRIMACK: As I said, I don't take a personal God seriously, at least in my rational self. So I don't think it makes a lot of sense to imagine that there's some divine order of human affairs that is pushing us in one direction and not another direction. On the other hand, there certainly are strong effects of the environment, including the human situation, that do push the development of the Earth in certain directions. None of this absolves humans of responsibility to choose wisely.

CLAYTON: Is this difficulty in thinking of a God who's active in the world something that's changed historically? Is it difficult to imagine such a God because we know what we do about the physical universe? Might it have made more sense in 1492?

PRIMACK: Sure. Before Galileo much less was known. Galileo is an excellent case. He was a religious Christian, no question about it. I mean he professed to be and there's no reason to think he wasn't.

CLAYTON: And the Book of Nature?

PRIMACK: That's what I'm thinking about. Galileo said there are two ways to study God, you can read the Bible, or you can read the Book of Nature. And it was an article of religious faith that they are not in contradiction. If they seemed to be in contradiction, you're just misinterpreting one or the other. The Book of Nature is basically how God works in the world. As a modern scientist I would say, the physical laws. Does that mean that God has to be actively involved, in other words, performing miracles all the time? Newton thought so because he saw lots of problems with his picture. For example, why do the planets all orbit in the same direction in the same plane?

CLAYTON: God was his epicycle.

PRIMACK: Effectively, yes. Galileo, as far as I can remember, never made any allusion to such a role for God, and neither did Newton, as far as I know, except in his private correspondence.

CLAYTON: So that makes them very much like a physicist working today; not wanting to have a God mingling in what's a pretty good physical explanation.

PRIMACK: Yes. And we're all Galileans. Galileo's the one who really invented the approach of modern physicists. He was standing on the shoulders of some important predecessors, but he's the one who basically established the pattern, and in many respects he was more of a modern scientist than Newton.

CLAYTON: Judaism, Islam and Christianity share a belief in human beings as persons, beings with moral responsibility, with freedom, with a special capacity for relationships with God. How do you see this notion of the human being as a person fitting in with contemporary theory and the physical sciences?

PRIMACK: It fits fine. Except I have a little concern with the last phrase, "the special capacity for relationship with God." But if you see that special relationship as perceiving how the universe works, as reading God in the Book of Nature – but as a participant in all of this, not just as an outsider – then I don't have any problem with that part either.

As a scientist, and particularly a physicist, what I try to do is to develop a mental picture of how the world works. And the thinking is to a great extent pictorial and mathematical, but mathematical in a frequently rather geometric sense. And the thing that's special about a picture is that you're used to seeing the whole thing at once. It's this all-in-one aspect that I'm trying to suggest by using the word picture.

CLAYTON: Holistic thinking?

PRIMACK: Yes. And that's very much in line with the way mystics think, according to standard mystical writings. In fact I like to think that there's sort of a dichotomy between the fundamentalist way of thinking on the one hand, which is very much rooted in a text, and the mystical way of thinking on the other hand, which is rooted in an experience, and often a visual experience. But when science is dead, when it's not being developed, then there's a real danger of it being converted into some sort of fundamentalist textbook.

CLAYTON: Your focus within religion is much more on the ethical than the metaphysical. I wonder how human beings as morally responsible entities fits in, say, for somebody who knows about evolutionary biology and appreciates our similarity to higher primates.

PRIMACK: I don't see any contradiction at all there. Remember that I quoted Einstein as saying that if you don't believe in a personal God, then you can't derive your morality from that. Morality has to come from the culture, from the education of the young. I think that's probably true and I'm worried about it. Although I think it worked okay with me, and frankly I think it's worked okay in my family, it doesn't seem to work very well among the general public. I'm not sure what the right answer is for other people. Maybe it is important to have a theistic, personal God, reinforcing personal morality. But I'm not comfortable with that way of thinking. I don't see a necessity to derive moral precepts from a theory of God. In the Jewish tradition morals are taught, in the family, in society, and it seems to work okay. The moral stuff is presented as: this is what you're supposed to do, the commandments. Judaism has a beautiful idea, *mitzvot*, the joy of obeying the commandments.

Moral precepts could very well have arisen through evolution, first in a biological sense and then in a cultural sense. I don't see any reason to think that they arose any other way, and that doesn't make me the least bit uncomfortable.

CLAYTON: Would it matter if it became crystal clear that humans evolved in a way that we fully understood out of other higher primates, and that there was no qualitative difference between us and the other life forms? Would that be bad news from a religious perspective?

PRIMACK: Not for me. In fact I think it's almost certainly true that humans evolved from apes. This obviously really bothers fundamentalists, but it doesn't bother me in the slightest. But the existence of human language and culture is a qualitative difference between us and all other animals on Earth. Adam named the animals, not vice versa.

CLAYTON: Okay, how about consciousness? Is that a sign of a difference? Is that theologically significant? Meaning the person conscious of himself or herself as a moral being, aware and able to think about his thinking?

PRIMACK: Well it's certainly true that only humans seem to have consciousness. To the extent that animals have self-awareness, it's of a lower grade. Maybe you've heard of the work of my cousin, David Premack, on language and chimpanzees. David was able to teach chimps many things. But he and his students never succeeded in teaching the chimps a personal pronoun, the pronoun that refers to something different if you say it or if I say it. Chimps had no trouble learning many words that always meant the same thing, independent of who used them, but they never got that.

CLAYTON: Are the differences between humans and other primates religiously significant, in your sense of religion?

PRIMACK: Certainly, to the extent that I try to have this relationship with the universe as a theoretical physicist, it depends on my being conscious. On the other hand, I think it's important to appreciate our cultural debt. The amount of material in our genes would fill an encyclopedia. The amount of material in our heads fills libraries. It's those libraries that bloom, not the little bit that's stored in our genes. Of course, we only differ slightly from chimpanzees in the content of our genes. But the libraries set us completely apart.

11 Charles Townes

Testing Faith, Wrestling with Mystery

In the early 1940s, Charles Townes worked on a top secret Bell Labs project to develop radar for WWII bombers. His suspicions that the wavelength chosen by his superiors would be lost in the water vapor in the humid Pacific combat theater were justified, and that particular radar model was of little value. However, that research inspired Townes to focus on the then unexplored relationship between microwaves and molecules, leading to discoveries in physics and chemistry, and to his textbook on microwave spectroscopy. This field also led to his invention of the maser. Along with a Bell Labs colleague, Townes, then at Columbia University, applied the same principle to light, winning the first US patents on the laser. In 1964, Townes shared the Nobel Prize with two Russian researchers for advances in the field of quantum electronics.

Townes received his PhD from the California Institute of Technology in 1939. After his stints at Bell Labs and Columbia University, Townes served as vice president and director of research at the Institute for Defense Analysis in Washington, D. C. In 1961, he was appointed professor of physics at Massachusetts Institute of Technology, where he later became provost. In 1967 he moved to the University of California at Berkeley to concentrate on astrophysics. There, in 1981, he chaired the commission that convinced President Reagan not to field fleets of MX missiles. Later, switching his attention to radio and infrared astronomy, Townes helped discover the presence of stable molecules in outer space. Now in his mid-eighties, Townes is University Professor of Physics, Emeritus, at the University of

California at Berkeley, where he continues to supervise astronomy graduate students.

Describing himself as a non-doctrinaire Christian, Townes prays daily and studies the Bible, considering it to be historical evidence of Christianity's power.

CHARLES TOWNES: I'm a Protestant, but I'm not a sectarian. As a child I was brought up a Baptist and I've been a member of almost every Protestant group in the United States including Episcopalian, Methodist and Presbyterian. I'm presently a member of the Congregational Church. Generally I go to the church I feel to be the best in my particular locality.

PHILIP CLAYTON: Was it ever difficult for you to integrate your life as a scientist and your religious life?

TOWNES: No, I never had trouble fitting them together. I was brought up in the South, where most people tend to be literal in their interpretation of the Bible, but my parents were understanding and fairly liberal and so when there were questions about the Bible, which there were, why, they generally agreed with me.

CLAYTON: If I'd been a graduate student with you, and an atheist, and I had said, "Isn't it obvious that our work as physicists excludes God's meddling in the world? He certainly doesn't show up in the equations?" how would you have answered?

TOWNES: I'd have explained that the equations may not be complete, that there is a great deal we don't yet understand. And there are inconsistencies within science itself, yet we continue to believe it.

CLAYTON: Do you see differences between the attitudes of the religious believer and the scientist? Are they contradictory? Complimentary? Or do you see them as closely related?

TOWNES: "The religious believer" refers to so many different types of people. Some feel that the two subjects are sharply divided and cannot be united. They may take both approaches seriously, but not believe they can be united. There is a very, very wide variety of views. It's not surprising to find almost anything. There are dogmatic religious persons and dogmatic scientific persons.

I regard science as trying to understand the structure and the operation of the universe, whereas religion tries to understand the purpose of the universe. Of course, those two things have to be closely related. In fact, I think religion and science are more similar than we generally give them credit for. Each requires human nature and the human mind to understand it. They both depend on evidence, which may be a scientific experiment, or experience, or history. We look at the evidence and consider it and try to build a consistent picture. We also have intuitions about how some things strike us or how we think they ought to be in order to be attractive and simple and understandable and so on. And we have to make postulates. We can't really prove anything firmly, so we make the most sensible postulates – we think we do anyhow – and we look at the observations and try to decide what is there. My approach to both science and religion is broadly very similar. And I think that as we understand more, the two will grow closer together.

CLAYTON: Are you sympathetic, then, to interpretations of science that focus on the role of personal knowledge or intuition?

TOWNES: I wouldn't say I'm particularly sympathetic to that. I think one needs to understand intuitions and human attitudes, and be objective about them, too. I would not shy away from being objective.

CLAYTON: Your view still challenges an older view of science that might have said that we have fully objective knowledge that we can get through purely objective techniques.

TOWNES: I would challenge that completely. Actually, that claim itself is not objective because we know that we have to base our thoughts on assumptions and postulates, which are not themselves provable.

CLAYTON: And you've already cited intuition, such as the intuition of beauty or simplicity.

TOWNES: Yes, many people have pretty fixed ideas of what the universe ought to be like, based on these intuitive things. Scientists who are quite a-religious do, and religious people do, too. There is something to intuition as a way of getting knowledge, but I wouldn't give it any absolute quality.

CLAYTON: Does your view of religion have a larger place for reason or observation or even testing than the traditional view might have held?

TOWNES: In general, I believe analysis and thought and testing of religion are good things. I see no reason why science should not eventually address what we might consider now non-quantitative, non-reproducible things. Science should go further and further, as far as it can go. Maybe there will be a limit, but I don't think we can define now where it will be. I hope science will eventually lead us on to knowledge about the aesthetic, religious and social realms that are so important to us.

Some religious people might argue that it destroys the nature of faith if you're trying to test it. But I don't think it necessarily does. My inclination is to say I believe that the supernatural and the natural will come together. What we regard as natural will include an increasing amount of information and understanding.

CLAYTON: How, then, do you understand the faith part? Clearly, in your view, it doesn't mean don't test, don't question, accept everything on blind authority.

TOWNES: No, no, it doesn't. There are cases where we can't test something and we can't prove it, and so we have to have faith. Again, the faith scientists have is so fundamental and all pervasive that most don't realize it is faith. We have faith that the universe follows reliable laws, that the universe is not ruled by many different kinds of conflicting laws, that the physical laws are real. We also have faith that the human mind can understand many of these laws. And it's that kind of faith that makes us willing to work at research and moves us to try to understand. If we expected things to be episodic and arbitrary, why, then there'd be no point in our trying to do science at all. The faith that scientists have is not that different from believing in one reliable God.

CLAYTON: So when we look more closely, we'll find that just as the role of reason in religion could be much larger than people have sometimes thought, the role of faith in science is much more pervasive than has been assumed?

TOWNES: Faith is crucial in science. And of course values are essential to science, too. It's very common to say, "Science has no sense of values." Well, science has a tremendous sense of values. Truth, for example, is pre-eminent. People who don't speak the truth, or who are not willing to face the truth, well, they're just out of the picture. Furthermore, the scientist, I think, has a very real sense of beauty. There is beauty in our universe and the scientist senses that, and you'll find it in the statements of many great scientists. Of course, Keats says, "Beauty is truth and truth beauty." There is the beauty of an equation and the generality of laws and so on.

CLAYTON: Given the strength of the parallels, how would you characterize the difference between faith in the two spheres, if any?

TOWNES: Well, the general scientific tenets in the physical sciences are much easier to test. If one goes to the social sciences, in some cases it's very difficult to make clear-cut tests. As one gets more and more into human factors, it becomes increasingly difficult. In the case of religion it's very difficult, but not impossible. In religion we generally replace what we think of as scientific tests with experience. Clearly, experience is like scientific observation. I can go out in the field as a naturalist and make scientific observations and see how birds behave and say, "I know how a mockingbird behaves and this may be why it behaves the way it does." So we may observe humans and humanity through history and through our personal experiences, and through the experiences of others – these are all observations that are in some sense experiments. The Bible is also a tremendous record, a historical record of evidence of how people behave, what religion does, what happens to certain points of view and so on. That's a tremendous evidential record and so is all history. We're not controlling the situation the way we might in physics, but we're observing and making deductions. We look at history, we look at our friends, we look at ourselves. We think about it. We use what logic we can. Those are the common experiments of a religious view.

CLAYTON: Do you think experiment could ever falsify your Christian belief?

TOWNES: Yes. Some say that their beliefs are absolute and never to be changed. I would say, no, we understand imperfectly.

And I think if you read the New Testament, certainly the disciples and the letters and so on, you get the view that they don't assume that they know everything perfectly. They're advising each other.

CLAYTON: So the process of falsification might extend to many of the doctrines that I, as a Protestant, once held and later felt were unjustified by the data? Say, an attitude about races or about men and women?

TOWNES: Yes. One shouldn't veer off of the possibility of testing any of those things and changing one's opinion. You mentioned racism and women and you find in the Bible a defense of slavery and the inferior positions of women and a variety of other practices that we don't accept now.

CLAYTON: Could a Christian justifiably become convinced that his belief in, say, Jesus as the Christ, was falsified for him?

TOWNES: Well, at that point he'd no longer be Christian. But I would not rule out the possibility of one's changing his opinion of the meaning of Jesus and his life. Anything we think we know is subject to examination. Now, that will be different from the overtly stated views of some Christians, of course.

CLAYTON: Are there disanalogies in the nature of the scientific sphere and the religious sphere?

TOWNES: Well, I certainly think we ought to have the pursuit of truth in both spheres. They're closely connected and I wouldn't make any clear-cut separation, but there certainly is a difference of emphasis. I think they're growing closer together all the time. For example, one question science and religion approach differently is: What was the beginning? Scientists tend to believe that the universe, not necessarily just our universe but some kind of structure, was always here and was always the same. Well, we know from the Big Bang that our own universe hasn't always been the same, and perhaps there are lots of other universes. We may be just one of a random sample of things that really has always been the same. Science is continually rebuffed in its thoughts about what the beginning implies. On the other hand, it seems very easy for the religious person to just say, "God did it." They never ask who made God. How did God get started? That's not considered an appropriate question in most religions. The religious assumption of God is very much like the scientist's assumption that there was something here that's just always been the same. And so you don't have to face how it got started. So even in that case there is remarkable similarity.

CLAYTON: Physics may presuppose an arrow of time, but Christian belief has classically presupposed a telos, direction, or goal built into the universe or brought about by God's subsequent involvement with the universe. What are the areas of overlap between work in contemporary physics and astrophysics and this question of destiny and purpose?

TOWNES: There is increasing and impressive evidence that our universe has some very special characteristics that make our kind of life possible. And that goes back to the more basic question of why the universe is as it is. We know that the Big Bang had particular characteristics. We know the laws of physics have particular characteristics. We know that the initiation of life on Earth came at a particular time and so on. There are a lot of special circumstances – this has become much clearer to us as time has gone on – which allow for life. One could claim that that makes it clear that there's a plan. And if there is a plan, there must be an intelligence with a purpose and so on. On the other hand, a non-believing scientist could claim that it's just an accident that it turned out this way, and that there are many universes and most of them don't produce this kind of life, but that if you have an infinity of them, why, there'll be at least one that turns out this way.

CLAYTON: How do you respond to that many-universes argument?

TOWNES: I can't argue that it's untrue because there is no way of testing it. If someone wants to believe it, it's okay with me. I don't find it a particularly pleasing explanation, but I can't throw it out completely either. I hope we will get some better understanding about why the physical constants are what they are. Maybe there's some logic or some necessity in it that we can dig out at some point. Or maybe we can show that these are created randomly and that there are many different universes. And I think addressing the questions of why our universe turned out the way it did, why the laws of physics and the physical constants and so on are what they are, ought to be among the goals of science. Those are valid subjects for further examination. I'm not so sure we'll solve those questions, but I certainly believe we'll know more about them in time.

CLAYTON: So it seems to you highly improbable that fundamental constants and laws would be such that life would arise. And if multiple universes are not taken as an out, then the hypothesis of intelligent design is an extremely attractive explanation of what we find. Is that your position?

TOWNES: I'd have to put some caveats on your use of "improbable." If there are fundamental reasons why the physical constants have to be just the way they are, then it may be highly probable. On the basis of what we presently know, one might guess that it is highly improbable. But there is a lot that we don't know. Many scientists believe that any planet similar to Earth, with the same chemical composition and so forth, is obviously going to develop intelligent life. They think the probabilities are very high. Again, I would have to say we still don't know. We don't know the processes by which life initially formed. We can attribute a great deal of the development of life to evolution, certainly, but the initial formation of the first self-duplicating cell, we don't know how that happened at all. And so we cannot put any numerical probability on it except to say, "It happened once, why shouldn't it happen again?"

CLAYTON: So, given that we have no adequate theory to explain how you get self-reproducing cells out of the primal soup, the hypothesis of God's creative activity remains scientifically viable?

TOWNES: I wouldn't put it that way. An atheist would say, "There's no reason to suppose that God did this just because we don't know how it was done." On the other hand, it certainly leaves that possibility open. The atheist might say, "God is just an assumption. Why is that a viable explanation? I can just assume life formed. Why do I have to assume God? Assuming God is just as problematic as assuming that life just formed."

CLAYTON: Is the question of the origin of life an evidential stale-mate? Does the physical, or proto-biological, evidence allow for two radically different interpretations?

TOWNES: There are not just the two possibilities: one that life is highly probable and automatically forms, and the other that God put it all together himself in some special way. As I see it, life may be very improbable, but it did happen and it happened in accordance with physical laws, and physical laws are laws that God made. We need not call on a special action of God for it to happen, even if it is highly improbable.

That raises another question: To what extent do we allow God to act in our universe in some way that's outside of the physical laws? First I would say that we don't yet know phys-ical laws well enough to say what's inside and what's outside of them. But our current laws, as we understand them, allow no room for separate action by God. Things are not determin-istic; nevertheless there is no room for some superimposed outside force coming in and affecting things. That doesn't trouble me as a religious person because I know that there are a lot of things we just don't understand yet. It may be there and we just don't understand it. So, for me, it's not a problem – it's an interesting puzzle, but not a problem. Of course an atheist would say, "Well, if there's no reason to think that God can take any action, what good is He?"

CLAYTON: Some scientist-theologians have speculated that if there are areas of the physical world that are essentially inde-terminate, divine action at that level would be possible. That would break no scientific laws. Some suggest quantum physics as such an area. Would you be sympathetic to that approach?

TOWNES: Well, I wouldn't be unsympathetic. But it's not true. One of the first well-known proponents of that view was Arthur Compton. When quantum mechanics first came along, he felt that the uncertainty principle allowed room for God. Einstein himself, and many other scientists, felt that there had to be some hidden forces, not necessarily God, but some kind of hidden forces that were determining things. But we have experiments now, based on Bell's theorem, which say that within the logic that we understand there are no hidden forces. And so our present laws don't leave any room for arbitrary, external action.

CLAYTON: Suppose the theologian said, "I don't mean external forces. I mean some sort of inner power, where probability states are resolved in one direction or the other by a purpose that underlies the universe, whom I call God."

TOWNES: That would be a hidden force that could affect quantum mechanical probability. And, according to present tests, there seems to be no place for one.

CLAYTON: Even if it were done in such a way that the overall probability distributions came out as expected, but individual cases might be resolved in one direction or the other?

TOWNES: Physics does not allow that. People also talk about chaos. They think chaos allows a lot of different things to happen that we can't figure out and so, maybe there's room for God there. As I see it, from the point of view of science, that's not valid either. Chaos simply means that the situation is too complicated for us to know all the variables and calculate outcomes. That doesn't invalidate the determinacy of classical mechanics, nor the indeterminacy of quantum mechanics. It doesn't change the laws, it doesn't mean that there's any new force involved. It just says that it's difficult for us to predict outcomes.

CLAYTON: It sounds to me like the classical perspective of Christianity – of God being present and active in the universe, giving purpose, guiding and acting providentially – is in trouble.

TOWNES: Well, certainly some forms of it, yes.

CLAYTON: Is there a sense of loss of the God who was once so present and active in the world?

TOWNES: Well, I think some people see it that way, yes, that science has sort of replaced God. But I don't think that's a necessary view. Look at revolutions in physics; let's say quantum mechanics in particular since it completely revolutionized physical thinking. What we thought was a completely deterministic world is not deterministic, and Newton's laws were changed, from a philosophical point of view, quite completely. Nevertheless, we still teach Newtonian physics in the universities. We still use it all the time – it's valid under a wide variety of circumstances. And so, in it's own sphere it's still quite usable and correct. It's a good approximation that fits our observations. And yet, philosophically, it's completely wrong.

Now, religious beliefs as they stand may involve some very basic misunderstandings, but they may still have a kind of validity in their own sphere. And in our present lives they still have an operational legitimacy that is quite right, just like Newtonian laws, even though basically our views may change completely. I would say, let's live by the best things we know now – hopefully we'll learn more. Operationally this is the best thing we know and it seems to work, so let's go forward with it. We don't have to assume that everything has to be consistent.

CLAYTON: You are saying that you can't make your entire religious belief dependent upon the current state of physics. We don't know that there won't be another revolution as big as the quantum revolution. We don't know that our understanding of biology won't be completely transformed. If you have religious belief, if you have a sense of a relationship with God, you can preserve that. If you have a sense of God as active in the world, you can continue to believe that, despite the contemporary deterministic sense that there's no physical place for God to do anything.

TOWNES: That's more or less right. Another example is our sense of free will. Science acknowledges no free will in the usual sense at all. And yet, I believe I have free will. I sense it very strongly; I think almost every other individual does. We're not completely free, but somehow we sense we have free will. In much the same way, I sense the presence of God and His influence. I was once in the laboratory and Professor Lamb, who was a great skeptic, came around and said, "Charlie, has God ever helped you in the laboratory?" I said, "Yes. I think He has." He couldn't take that. He was so astounded he just didn't proceed to ask me how. That is a little harder to explain. But I think there is something in it. In any case, I have this very strong sense, as many other people do, of God's presence.

CLAYTON: We share so much genetic matter with the other higher primates, and we so well understand the process of evolution of higher life forms. Yet, Christian tradition says that human beings are morally responsible, free, with a special capacity for a relationship with God. Is there a tension there?

TOWNES: No, not to me. Clearly we can write and speak in more complex ways than the other anthropoids. So there is a difference. That doesn't mean there's not a lot of similarity. Apes can think. They can maybe even use language a little. But we have much more responsibility for what the world is like than do the apes. Apes can't do much to influence the world; they do eat fruit and spread the seeds around. But humans affect the world drastically. In that sense we're sort of co-creators with God. So I would say there's a substantial difference. One could argue about whether it's quantitative or qualitative. But the quantitative difference is so great that I think, effectively, it becomes qualitative.

CLAYTON: Another way of putting the question is, do you think that the Christian today needs to say that humans have souls but apes don't?

TOWNES: I'd have to know what you mean by a soul. I presume you mean something that lives after the body is dead. That's a big question, of course. What is the nature of a soul? And then, in what sense does it live after the body is dead? And I think an increasing number of Christians have doubts about the nature of the afterlife as being personal and so complete and so on. So to say that humans have souls and apes don't is too extreme. I wouldn't say it's necessarily wrong, but I don't see any great logic in it either.

CLAYTON: The religious beliefs that you hold seem very responsive to the growth of knowledge in the sciences.

TOWNES: Let me say I expect both science and our understanding of religion to change with time. Religion has not changed nearly as rapidly as science has. Some religious people would say that's natural because it's more right to begin with. It doesn't need to change. That's not my view. I think if you wanted to be kind to religious views, you could say some of the statements of the Bible are right, but we're not interpreting them correctly. I wouldn't argue that they are always right or always wrong. I would say our understanding of the situation is undoubtedly incomplete. And as we understand more, then I think we'll read different things into those words.

CLAYTON: You seem to be calling for something like the classical
Christian virtue of humility on the part of both the scientist
and the religious person.

TOWNES: I would certainly ask for that, yes. And I think scientists
are increasingly humble, particularly physicists, because
they've been through revolutions and they recognize in very
hard, quantitative ways, where they haven't understood things
and where they still don't understand things. Some of the
other sciences, which are not as exact yet, don't have the challenge that physics has had of saying, "Well, gee, we were
really quite wrong."

CLAYTON: It's clear from this discussion that your goal is to find a
way of integrating physical results with religious belief and
making religious belief responsive to scientific developments.

TOWNES: I wouldn't call it my goal. I would say my belief is that
they must, in the long run, be much better integrated. If we
understand either one well enough, they will come closer
together. I believe they will overlap more and more. I would
like to see that, but I hesitate to use the word "goal" because
it suggests that I'm sure that that has to be right. And while I
believe that the two will overlap and, as we understand them
better, will grow closer together, I want to be open-minded
and responsive to whatever we learn. If we learn, in fact, that
they are completely separate in some way, why, okay, I would
like to know that. But that's not my expectation.

CLAYTON: A number of physicists have moved from experimental
questions to fundamental theoretical questions to a type of
reflection that would have to be called highly speculative. Paul
Davies, for example, writes books with titles such as *God and
the New Physics* and *The Mind of God*. Are you sympathetic
with that way of making the connection, namely, moving
from physics to metaphysics or religion?

TOWNES: In the past there have been a great many semi-religious
ideas and a lot of metaphysical speculation in science. If we
just go back to Einstein's theory that everything had to be
deterministic, that was a very common feeling. In this century,
many scientists have felt that the universe had to be always
constant. An expanding universe and a Big Bang were very
objectionable to many people. Many scientists have quite

recently thought, "Well, the universe has to be exactly closed, a flat universe." These are speculative ideas, or semi-religious, you might say. At least they are intuitive ideas that people have become very attached to. And I think to propose them as attractive or preferable and so on, is excellent. We ought to be looking at all the possibilities. But to insist that they must be right based on intuition or whatever is not something that I would support particularly. We should be careful to be clear about where we're thinking rigorously in terms of the science that most scientists will accept and where we're speculating. Not that there's necessarily a sharp line, but I think we need to be realistic. Speculation is generally, I think, a good thing, as long as we recognize it as speculation.

CLAYTON: A number of theorists suggest that the universe is evolving toward greater complexity, for instance. From there they go on to claim that there must be some sort of inherent tendency toward complexity, and they explain that by some sort of meta-law. To an outsider it is sometimes hard to separate what's good physics and what's religious zeal.

TOWNES: I agree, to some extent. I think one has to be cautious and I hope scientists will be clear about why they're saying something.

CLAYTON: On the other hand, some physicists refuse to speculate at all beyond the math and the hard evidence. Fermi, for instance, was famous for being very pragmatic. Here are the equations, here are the observations, and beyond that, everything's just speculation. Is there a justification, for you as a physicist, in being extremely skeptical about all theories about the nature of the physical world?

TOWNES: I wouldn't say I'm extremely skeptical. I try to be open-minded about speculation. If I can't disprove a speculative theory, it may be of some interest and may be attractive. On the other hand, I don't want to get locked in on that. I have to wait and see. Before committing, I've got to try to find out if an idea is really right.

Now, you mention complexity. Our physical laws are getting a little more complicated in the sense that we're adding new particles, we're adding new terms. Nevertheless, the physical laws are remarkably simple. What's complex, and sometimes too complex for us to understand, are the behaviors produced by a total addition of things. And yet one of the faiths of the scientist is that if you work hard enough at it, you will understand. So we keep working at it. I accept that faith. I don't know that it's true, but that's my basis of operation. You have to have some set of assumptions. My assumption is that the human mind can understand the world around us and that we should keep trying.

CLAYTON: Modern astronomers project different possible fates for the universe. Is one of these more convincing to you than the others? All but Steady State suggest that the conditions necessary for life will not be sustained forever. Does that have religious significance?

TOWNES: Actually, I think the expansion of the universe is fairly well established. It's probably going to keep expanding and cooling down. But maybe it'll go out and stop, or maybe it'll go out and collapse again. In either of those cases, you might be inclined at first to think that human civilization will be gone. But I don't think that's necessarily so. Given the time involved, we may be able to be a little smarter in the future, in the next billion years or so, and move to other stars. I'm sure that's hard; it'll take a long time. But the human race could still exist by moving to other planets and other stars as they get cooler and more hospitable. With appropriate nuclear energy, we might be able to bring some cold masses together and start a few new stars, even. I don't think one should discount that possibility. It's only the collapse that would finish us off, and that may not be for another fifty billion years or so.

CLAYTON: Do you draw inspiration from your own specific research and areas of specialization? Do they provide inspiration for your religious beliefs?

TOWNES: Witnessing the upset of firmly believed scientific assumptions is pertinent to religious belief. We mustn't oversimplify too much, we mustn't get caught in some scientific generalization that we think is attractive. So that's one aspect. The beauty of nature as we learn it through science, and as we learn it outside of science, I find quite inspirational and impressive. Then there are the parts of science such as cosmology which, I think, have really challenged scientific views as well as religious ones. They open things up and make one think. Cosmology is a remarkable field in that respect. It's a source of inspiration. I believe that biology is, or will be, too, because there is so much to learn there. Biological systems are fascinating and complex.

One of the things I've done since I've been here at Berkeley is to find molecules in interstellar space. People thought there weren't many molecules there. It turns out that there are a lot of them. And what does that have to do with religion? Well, in the long run, it gives us a source of material from which life can form. And our planet was formed out of those interstellar clouds, so we know right from the beginning it had complex, organic molecules, which may help our understanding of the origin of life. That has some bearing on religion.

CLAYTON: So it's not as if the discovery of the molecules provided a direct connection with any particular religious belief, but it helps build a fuller scientific picture which, as a whole, is inspiring to a Christian believer?

TOWNES: Yes, I would generally agree with that.

CLAYTON: And, for instance, when you talk about astrophysics, or cosmology and the inspiration it provides, is it such that Big Bang cosmology is more inspirational than the Steady State theory, more of a support for the religious belief in the creation by God than its competitor?

TOWNES: I think both are fascinating. I wouldn't say that one is inconsistent with the creation by God. But the Big Bang is much more suggestive of a unique time in the universe when things were forming. And it fits a little more clearly into the story of *Genesis* and the story of the creation that most religions have.

CLAYTON: I take your choice of the word "suggestive" to be saying that this is not a natural theology or a proof of some sort, with natural theology being evidence for the agency of God in the world.

TOWNES: No. I would hesitate on the word "proof."

CLAYTON: Are there any parts of your religious belief that have directed or guided or affected your own scientific work?

TOWNES: Well, in terms of anything very specific, the answer would be no. On the other hand, I think all of science, in a sense, comes from belief in order in the universe. That's part of scientific faith and that's part of the Judeo-Christian tradition, that there is one God, not random competing Gods. So from a very broad point of view I would say, yes, there is an effect. But from a more detailed point of view, the answer would be no, excepting the general values of the worthwhileness of life, the joy of life, the creativity of life. All of those things are part of my religious view.

12 Anne Foerst

Do Androids Dream of Bread and Wine?

Anne Foerst is professor for Computer Science and Theology at St Bonaventure University in Olean, NY. While involved with the Science and the Spiritual Quest program, she was Research Associate at the Center for the Studies of Values in Public Life at Harvard Divinity School and a researcher at the Artificial Intelligence Laboratory and director of the God and Computers project at the Massachusetts Institute of Technology. A Lutheran minister, Foerst served as the theological adviser to the scientists at MIT who are building intelligent robots. Unlike most efforts to create "intelligent" machines by filling their memories with factual information and other intellectual capacities, the MIT project seeks to create artificial intelligence the way humans build their own, through experience. Foerst and her colleagues insist that if the robot's "mind" is going to be recognizable to humans, its interface with the world must also be human-like, or, to use the project's phrase, "embodied." Hence the robots have body parts that resemble their human counterparts as closely as possible. They also have primary "parental" relationships and are raised like people from infancy up.

Foerst believes that a dialogue between AI and contemporary theology could bear tremendous fruit. Trying to recreate human characteristics in a machine requires a fundamental and rigorous examination of those characteristics themselves, including the elusive qualities we call spirit, dignity and rights. It is in these intangible areas that Foerst's expertise in the history and methods of the theology are engaged. At what point, she asks, will turning off an intelligent robot constitute murder? And at what point might it be appropriate to baptize a machine?

ANNE FOERST: In Germany we really have only two churches: Catholic and Protestant. I belong to the Protestant Church. And I belong to an area that I would say is more Lutheran oriented. So here in the US I find myself mostly represented by Lutheran Churches.

I studied theology for seven years and planned to become a minister. I never took the final course or became ordained; however, I took my first Church exam, so I'm a Master of Divinity and I've worked as a minister. I have worked as a ministry counselor, did a lot of sermons. I pretty much married all my friends and even baptized some of their children.

I have a feeling that in the US, Christianity often means very strong devotion to going to Church every Sunday. I am not this way. So when I say I am a very active Christian, I mean that I am a very spiritual person and feel myself often in contact with God. I also try to live my Christianity. But I'm not totally devoted to an outer life of Christianity where everything is service.

GORDY SLACK: Do you see your religious life as being rooted mostly in a spiritual association with Christianity, or with an ethical or theological affiliation? Or is this a false dichotomy?

FOERST: For me this is a false dichotomy. Ethics, for me, is always a consequence of what you are thinking and your spirituality. For instance, in my work at MIT, where we are currently building humanoid robots, and where you could raise a lot of ethical issues, of course I don't raise them. Because I think to be ethical and to follow certain ethical rules and to follow certain standards, you must have certain convictions about what humans are and what their value is. Since my evaluation of what it means to be human is influenced by my Christianity, I apply intrinsic value, personhood and dignity to all people. And this leads me to certain ethical consequences. But I always have trouble with people applying ethical rules to other people who do not share their assumptions about the world. I am of course rooted in Christianity, both in the spirituality and ethics, but only because I buy the assumptions – which my fellow researchers at MIT do not necessarily do.

SLACK: And so your ethics are the consequence of assumptions you share with other Christians?

FOERST: Yes, a consequence. And I have to say I do not share all of these assumptions. Many Christians seem to agree upon a certain ethical "program" including questions on abortion, homosexuality, et cetera. For me, the center of Christianity is the so-called "double law of love": you should love God and you should love your neighbor like yourself. These laws need to be constantly reinterpreted, but they are the guideline I attempt to arrange my life around.

SLACK: Would you please describe the Cog project, in its bare bones, so to speak? I have heard Cog has a head, a torso and two arms.

FOERST: Cog is an attempt to build a humanoid robot and to imitate a human newborn. It's a project of what is called "Embodied AI," which is a very new field within artificial intelligence which says that the body is crucial for intelligence. Intelligence, in classical AI, has always been considered separate from the body. It's always been reduced to cognition, to rational information processing et cetera. Embodied AI thinks that's not correct. We need a body. We need emotions. We need development. We need social interactions.

So, Cog is first of all built with a human-like body. And by human-like body, so far, you are right, we work with the parts you have described above, so it has no legs. We justify it by saying a newborn baby doesn't walk. It can move its head, for instance, exactly like a human can. It has to work with equilibrium forces to stay upright. It can move its arms exactly the way a human can. Its eyes, for instance, have a fovea, where it can see focused images in a very small range, and then it has a wide range camera where it can see unfocused, but very wide, which is exactly how the human eye works. We try to imitate as much as possible the human body in order to give Cog experiences that are as close to human experiences as possible. Cog also has a human likeness so that its interactions with humans will be as human-like as possible. We believe that artificial intelligence is only possible if we make the artificial intelligence system part of a community, if we treat it like a human. And to treat it like a human, we have to give it a body that we can interact with.

SLACK: And not just a keyboard.

FOERST: Exactly. The standard criterion for intelligence for us is that it's disembodied and it simulates the intelligence of a grown-up. But how should such a poor machine get this way? It doesn't have any development or life experience. Of course giving it these things is incredibly difficult and complex. We try a whole range of different technological projects at once in one single robot and we have to connect them and the robot has to learn to coordinate all these things. But we have coordinated the hands, the eyes and the ears, meaning that Cog can move its head toward noise. It can see motion and it reaches its hand towards motion. It can also get immediate input from its surroundings. For instance, it can play with a slinky because it can "feel" the weight on its hands and can react accordingly. No classic AI system could ever perform that way.

SLACK: Do you find yourself having parental impulses toward Cog?

FOERST: At the moment we have not gone this far yet. It's clear that Cog will have close connections to only three or four people.

SLACK: There is so much that goes on for a human infant that are, for lack of a better word, internal, and I don't just mean cognitive, but chemical and hormonal, too. How can you simulate those "experiences" that we don't directly observe?

FOERST: We can only really simulate what cognitive science gives us as insight. So we are working very closely with neurobiologists and developmental psychologists, and we have a lot of very good people at MIT. We meet once a week in the group called the Zoo, because so many exotic people are in there. And we often invite developmental psychologists and neurobiologists and other cognitive scientists, and talk with them about certain aspects of our work. They usually send us papers. We prepare questions of what we want to get out of the meetings and then they come and talk with us. Often, these interactions motivate us to write a certain program or do certain things.

In terms of what you were saying about hormones and chemicals in our body, in principle I agree with you. For instance, bio-body skin is different than metal. There is no question about that. But I hesitate to always focus on what is lacking. I don't want to imitate the typical argumentation against AI and especially against Cog, "but it does not have. this and that and therefore it cannot become human," because this argument can be easily overcome by scientific and techno-logical progress.

But in principle I agree with you, for instance: Cog doesn't experience growth. Then – and this shows my clear feminist critique of this whole project – Cog doesn't have a gender, which is impossible because every infant instantly has a gender and this gender marks from the beginning their indi-viduality and character.

SLACK: That was going to be my next question: How does sexu-ality factor into the formation of Cog's personality? It is obviously such a powerful part of early human experience.

FOERST: It doesn't. Yes, it's definitely lacking. But they've tried so much already; you can only do a certain amount at one time. Rodney Brooks always says he hopes to rebuild Cog again and again, adding something new each time. At the moment we are just trying to get the hardware running in a way so that it can coordinate its arms, its hands, its eyes, its ears and its body. In itself, that would be fantastic.

SLACK: How does this idea of intelligence as an emergent prop-erty of a physical body mesh with Christian theology?

FOERST: This, for me, is the interesting thing. Classical theology always tried to interpret the *Imago Dei*, humans being created in the image of God, as those features we have that distinguish us from anyone else: intelligence, or cognition, or whatever. But I am perfectly comfortable with the idea that intelligence and self-consciousness and all these things are emergent phenomena. It brings us back more into Creation. Because we are smart and have self-consciousness, we took ourselves out of Creation and understood ourselves as something special. If studies show that you find self-consciousness in monkeys, that monkeys are cheating and so forth, then there is not that much of a difference between them and us. So if we give up this notion that intelligence is something special, God-given, but just an emergent phenomenon, we are forced to put ourselves back into the Creation. We become more modest. This is what I like about Cog. It can kind of support this notion.

SLACK: I'm sure many people see Cog as an expression of hubris, or arrogance, rather than of modesty.

FOERST: I don't know if you are familiar with the Golem tradition, the stories of the Jewish mystic, the Kabbalah, about artificial humans made from clay. There are several of them around, all written from the fourteenth to sixteenth centuries. I have read most of them. The Kabbalists, who built the Golems from clay, did this as a kind of service. For them it was a way of adoring God by mirroring His Creative powers. They said, "We are images of God and this means we got His creative powers. And so we can create ourselves." So, for them, the Golem and its construction was always more or less a form of prayer. I have no difficulty seeing Cog in that light. I think it is just amazing that people are trying to build such a thing. And in a way, we rediscover the greatness of God's creation every day: imagine, since 1993 several brilliant people have worked on this project, worked on it hard, and still every newborn is so much better and more sophisticated than Cog.

It gets problematic though, and this is why I like this project. Rodney Brooks invited me, as a theologian, to participate so that they don't try to do more than they actually can. They just say, "It's fascinating to build such a machine. We want to see how far we can go technologically." But the danger of those things is always that it then becomes hubris by promising more than is actually there. For instance, a lot of AI research promised to make people eternal, to give them eternal life. Which is, for me, clearly hubris and wrong: AI cannot do this. AI then tries to answer existential questions for which they are not responsible. But Rod really tries hard not to fall into this trap. This is the reason I have no trouble seeing Cog as a kind of mirror of God's creative powers.

SLACK: Can you imagine a time when one of Rodney Brook's versions of Cog should be baptized?

FOERST: I would have no trouble with this. He says that to me, but always adds that I shouldn't use water.

SLACK: I guess the question is whether the word would be "christened," in the sense of christening a ship, or "baptized." Would you want to break a bottle over it or drip water on its forehead?

FOERST: I think I would baptize it. This is the whole issue: that we are created in the image of God does not mean that God gave us intelligence and all this kind of stuff. Like I have said, AI tells us that the *Imago Dei* should not be equated with "intelligence," "rationality" or "reason." In my opinion, *Imago Dei* just means that God in creating us started a relationship with us, and separated us from the rest of creation by starting and maintaining this relationship with us – but this separation is not because of some features we have. If the *Imago Dei* is purely and only relational, then I have no trouble thinking that Cog might have a relationship with us and then with God, too, at some point. If it develops the way it does, then Cog will ask at some point, "Where do I come from?" and "What is the meaning of my life?"

Let's look at values like dignity and personhood and things like this. My research group would say that these are emergent phenomena and therefore can be reduced in principle to some kind of mechanistic and functional properties. But from my Christian point of view I would say, "No, these are attributes we give to humans because we believe that they are created in the image of God." So, because it's an attribute, given to us as a gift, we can give this attribute to Cog at some point, too. So, you see, Cog doesn't take away our dignity. Quite the contrary, at some point we might have to assign it dignity, too.

SLACK: There is a sense in which our dignity certainly comes from our mutual recognition of it. But there is also a sense in which we have to deserve that dignity. You can't invent something and give it dignity simply because you've decided to.

FOERST: No. I perfectly agree with this. I mean there must be something there first. When I say that, more provocatively, it's really more that I don't see a qualitative difference in principle between the machine and us, from this respect.

I don't think that dignity is just a concept we give to one another. I mean that is really where the Christian speaks. I think it's a concept that is given to us by God first. That act of creation and affirmation is the source of all concepts of dignity and intrinsic value. I think that all the big religions pretty much agree on this.

SLACK: The mechanism that God uses to instill us with dignity could be described by sociologists, or psychologists, or neurologists in a mechanistic way that might include this kind of mutual recognition, and still would be attributable to God as its source.

FOERST: Yes, but you know, when you talk about the sociologist or psychologist's explanation, they are mostly reductionist. When they want to explain the world in a reductionist manner, I mean it's their problem. But you first have to buy into reductionism to believe their explanations. And reductionism has a lot of religious elements in it, and it often becomes a belief. For instance, the neurobiologist V. S. Ramachandran, at the University of California at San Diego, found a correlation between religious experience and certain neural activity. There's a pretty clear relationship between these neural activities and ecstasy, you know, religious unity and mystic experiences. A lot of reductionists say, "See! It's all in the brain and there is no God." And I say, "Wait a moment. This doesn't say anything about the existence of God." So there is a correlation between neural activity and experience? So what? So sociologists and psychologists are right to say it also needs the community – Christianity knows this too – but they cannot say, "And that's all."

SLACK: In the meeting of the cosmologists for the CTNS Science and the Spiritual Quest program, in a discussion about the multiple universe theories, someone posed the possibility that a new universe could be created, hypothetically, by a human being with the right equipment. Of course there wouldn't be any access to it so its relevance to us would be dubious. But this train of thought raises the question for me: if we could create animal-like or human-like intelligence, could we also create something that we would be tempted to call god-like intelligence? Could there emerge a field of AG, or "Artificial God?"

FOERST: I don't know. I think it depends on how you define God. When you define God as something that is the ultimate intelligence, then you might be able to do it. But I'm probably too much rooted in Christianity. For me, first of all, God is a personal God. And second of all, my recognition of God is totally dependent on God's revelation to me first. So I am not able to recognize God just because I look into nature, or I look into intelligence and all this kind of thing. The German Protestant Church already has rejected this notion of what is called natural theology because they said it leads, in the long run, to this whole tradition of arguments Ludwig Feuerbach and others have formulated. Feuerbach was a philosopher in the last century who said, pretty much, that God is a projection, that we project everything which is good and which is fine into God. We take the extreme of every good quality and make God out of this; God thus is just a projection of our desire for the ultimate truth and the absolute best and nothing more. No one had really thought about that before Feuerbach and everyone said, "Oh my God! He might be correct." Protestant theology reacted by saying, "Yes, that's the reason natural theology is not possible. We do not recognize God in this world, otherwise we would be too much in danger to project and to create a God we want. Therefore, God has to start a relationship with us first." If I take this concept seriously, and I do, then I cannot rebuild God. Because when I have this sort of relationship with God, it's still too big for me. And it's also transcendent, so it is not part of this world, so I couldn't express it in terms of this world, or materials of this world. Furthermore, this God is by definition a paradox: God is all-powerful and compassionate, an abstract force and a personal God. If you try to build a system bottom-up, you might be able to create some features that would help to come up with paradoxes in the end – but systems of that size like this idea of God cannot be planned. It seems therefore unreasonable from both a Christian and a systems point of view.

SLACK: I suppose though – going out further than I ought to on a limb of hypothesis – if you were able to create an alternative universe, that is, a parallel universe to which there was no access, into which you could put alternative intelligences that you also created, there would be a way in which you, the scientist, would stand in that transcendent relationship to the organisms, or the machines or whatever, in that parallel universe. You would be the source of their being, not directly accessible to them, and also somehow permeating them.

FOERST: That's right. In principle that's absolutely right. So probably my God is also a kind of a being from another universe.

SLACK: So you couldn't create your own God, but you could create someone else's God.

FOERST: Yes, probably. Ultimately, it always comes back to a question of faith: you either believe that it's a big engineer or you believe that it's God. And you can neither prove the one nor the other. I think this is what the whole debate about religion and science is about. People try to prove that they are right and that the others are wrong. So naturalists try to prove that there is no God and that it's all crap. And Christians try to prove that there is a God. Neither side takes faith seriously enough. In my opinion it always comes down to a question of faith.

SLACK: Could we talk for a moment about how faith factors into your work as a scientist? In your typology of relationships between science and religion you lay out four different models: conflict, contrast, contact and confirmation. I gather that you operate in either the contact model or the confirmation model. Could you talk a little bit about that?

FOERST: In a way I reject all four models in the classical religion and science dialogue because I think they are all dependent on what I call Cartesianism. Both theologians and humanities people, especially in this century, followed the scientific track, believing in objectivity, believing in rationality and all these kinds of things. In dialogue between religion and science, especially in terms of cosmology and evolution, both sides argue exactly the same way.

SLACK: With the same assumptions?

FOERST: Yes. And the same technology, the same way of arguing, the same way of perceiving the world. They assumed that there were objective empirical facts. So there was really no difference between the two. In my work I have tried to create a different epistemology. Science has a valid way to try and prove its world view and science needs naturalism. Science needs materialism. Science has to try, for instance, to build Cog from purely materialistic laws. If they conclude that self-consciousness is given by God, they would be making a mistake. They would betray themselves and they would have to give up the project and would never find out how far we can go with our current technology. Scientists have to believe in the validity of materialism. They have to say, "For my work, I need to assume the hypothesis that everything is materialistic!" which is a statement of faith.

Theologians, on the other hand, have to do the same thing. My whole perception of the world is built on the assumption that there is a God. Sorry, I can't prove it empirically, it's just my faith. And that's the thing that keeps me running. And therefore I can attribute dignity to people, and I can say that there are problems with cloning humans. But both ways of approaching the world, the scientific and the theological, are equally valid. And both are lacking in certain ways. And in the end we can only come together if we admit these elements of faith, and if we both admit the differences between our work and then we can to talk to one another and see what we can come to. For instance, in a paper in which I talk about Cog as an image of God, I only came to this because I gave up this notion that the *Imago Dei* is something that is objectively there, empirically proven. I gave this up and I was suddenly able to enormously enrich this whole concept. And I was able to give this back to AI people and they looked at this paper and said, "Hey, you are right. That's really interesting." I think that's the way to make the dialogue.

SLACK: You're an unusual person in that you've refined both of these aspects of yourself; your science has reached a high level of refinement and so has your theology. What kind of an internal dialogue goes on when the scientist in you speaks to the theologian in you, or to the religious person in you? Or am I implying a schism that doesn't really exist?

FOERST: No, it's a really good question. What I'm doing, of course, is always highly biographically motivated. I was born with this faith. When I was a child I had a strong faith in God. As an adolescent I was a radical atheist, which is pretty normal. And I went to theological seminary being an atheist. I wanted to find reasons for my atheism; I didn't know if it was correct or not. So I have this whole debate in myself. It took a long time before I realized that when I'd look to the notion of God from a typical rational, scientific way of thinking, I would always come to a dead end: "There is no God. There cannot be a God. It is totally crap."

But I was also suffering because a part of me knew that this was wrong. I knew there was a God, but I just couldn't put my finger on how I knew it. I just couldn't show it empirically, and all the people around me told me that it was crap. I knew God existed, but my knowledge was beyond the empirical evidence of science. I think this was the thing that kept me going. Then I started studying computer science, which I found fascinating. The problem was with my theologian fellows. I didn't like some of them that much, and I loved the computer scientists. I got along with them so well. But at the same time, they were all atheists and they thought I was totally bogus to believe in God. So I think it had a lot to do with people I was related to and I liked and could make jokes with, people I lived with. And today it's much more settled. I'm working on these questions all day long. But I still take my own concept of doubt very seriously. It's still very often that I sit there and look at Cog and see when Cog makes eye contact with me and learns something new in interaction with me. And I am standing there and say to myself, "Well, maybe we are just machines." Then, instead of just rejecting this thought, I try to go to the very edge. I try to ask myself, "What would it mean if we were?" Then I think about all the ethical consequences of proving that we are just machines.

SLACK: Let me ask you about the tools you use to examine what it would mean, ethically, if we were to discover or acknowledge that we are machines. Are they tools borrowed from your theological tool belt? Or do you take them from the tool belt of the scientist?

FOERST: Well, I think that the ability to doubt is a theological tool. Because when I believe in a God who is faithful to me, I can doubt this God and God will not give me up. This is the classical Job approach. Job says, "Okay, you are there and you are an asshole." I love Job, by the way. And that's the approach I take. I take the faithfulness of God seriously, and I know that God will not let me down even though I let God down. And so I can jump into this hole of doubt or of materialism knowing that there is still something that helps me, which is a very theological concept. But then, when I am in this hole, I proceed more scientifically. I validate all the theories I know about cognitive science, about neurobiology, all these explanations of phenomena like self-consciousness. There are computer scientists who are already pretty much able to build models of and simulate self-consciousness. So I use all the knowledge I have to kind of create a model in my mind that is entirely mechanistic. And when I am at that point, then I switch back to theology and look at what would happen if this pure materialist model of humankind were the correct one. In terms of human interaction, how would we react to one another if this were true? Here I am very much supported by the affiliation I have with the Center for the Study of Values in Public Life, at Harvard. We did a lot of analysis of mechanistic and functionalistic values in marketing strategies and economic theories. We found that most of the common theories, which are taught at most universities, including the Kennedy School (we are working together with the Kennedy School), are based on this very reductionist, mechanistic model of humankind. And this clearly leads to a certain ethic – or non-ethic – that humans are the *Homo economicus*, that it's only win and lose, and no solidarity, and no money for the poor, and no social system and all this kind of stuff. So that's one aspect that is already there, but I also try to go on to what would happen in interpersonal relationships. For instance, relationships would be reduced to sexuality because this is all that's there, right? And friendships would be reduced to: I use you and you use me. Relationships to children would be reduced to, "Well, okay, this is my offspring, be good to my genes." When I really go to extremes, I realize that this cannot work. And then I am pretty convinced that this is not true.

SLACK: I wonder if it is essential or an historical accident that we use the word "knowing" for both the kind of knowing that you felt as a child, and again as an adult, that God exists, and the way we use the word "knowing" to describe our confidence in the accuracy of a description of physical law, say. They just seem like such very different kinds of things.

FOERST: In Hebrew the word *jada* means "to recognize." And the word *jada* also means "to sleep with someone." But it's never meant in a just entirely sexual context, but always in the context of a really loving relationship. To recognize someone means to have sex with someone, in the whole sense of making love with someone. To recognize something in the scientific context always means to separate myself from this thing, to undergo a subject–object split. But the other notion of to recognize something is to become a part of this, to overcome the boundaries between me and the other. I think that's very much the difference between a theological recognition and the scientific recognition of, for instance, humans. I think you're right that a lot of confusion comes because we use the same word. On the other hand, a lot of confusion comes because people take their preferred method as the ultimate valid one and reject the others.

SLACK: But when you have someone for whom knowing is primarily in the divided subject–object use, and they are in conversation with someone who says they know that God exists, that could be a very baffling assertion. "How could you possibly know that God exists? What could you possibly mean by that?" Maybe what one really means by that use of "knowing" is something altogether different. But because of this linguistic coincidence, you walk down a path that requires evidence like that you would provide in a scientific proof.

FOERST: Yes. Because theologians don't want to admit that their knowledge is different. They have tried to buy this whole scientific package of objectivity and have tried to take this as the foundation for knowing. In my opinion, they give way too much up by doing this. And when I think about this whole creationist versus evolutionist debate, Ugh!— Actually, before I came into this country, I didn't even know that this debate existed.

SLACK: Yes, it's funny that the European scientists that I've talked to for this project have pretty much said, "What conflict

between evolution and the Creation story?" But Americans
are very aware of that tension.

FOERST: Yeah, but it's the same thing. Both sides have empirical
evidence, or think they have empirical evidence. And they
throw these arguments against one another and they don't
really listen. For me, I can happily say there is evolution and
there is God as a Creator. It's just a different form of knowing.

SLACK: On the other hand, there is a great temptation to create a
unified theory, especially a unified theory of your own experience. Probably, as you're saying, the only way to reach an
integrated perspective on the world is to engage in this kind of
dialogue, given that there are these different points of view.
But to ask the question, "What is the *real* origin of the
universe? How can I describe it in such a way that I don't
have to keep changing my hat?" is for some people very
powerful. I wonder if that begins to explain why there is this
almost fanatical kind of debate about which perspective is the
correct one, or which story is the right one to tell.

FOERST: I think you are absolutely right. For me, there is no such
a thing as a unified theory. I approach the world in stories and
this I have learned from Jesus. He described the world in
metaphors, parables and pictures. They are not necessarily
coherent, nor do they create a unifying theory about who we
are or what the world is. If they were unambiguous, theologians wouldn't have argued about their meaning for millennia.
I take this Jesuanic approach towards reality very seriously
but express it a little different. I've used some Gestalt concepts
to explain this. Gestalt problems express exactly this approach
towards reality: different people see different stories and a full
description of the picture is only possible if you put all
possible descriptions together and also include the people who
gave the explanations and their motivations for coming up
with this instead of that story, et cetera.

I can say there are stories that, for me, are definitely not
valid. But there are so many valid stories that are not
coherent. But they trigger different parts of who I am and why
I am here. And I'm not a coherent person. Here, we enter this
whole Biblical notion of sin as estrangement. Living in polarities and ambiguities, you cannot balance or overcome. This is

for me the whole notion of who we are. Actually, for St Paul, the attempt to overcome these polarities is the main sin. So, in this sense, the attempt to come to a unifying theory is the ultimate expression of sin; to not accept that the world is so manifold that we cannot put it into a theory, that we would reduce its beauty – I know this temptation for myself. It's so much easier. Everyone supports you; everyone agrees with you. But it cuts off so much richness of life. So the fact that there are no unifying theories actually is a gift. Imagine how boring it would be if we knew the unified theory.

SLACK: That it would be boring is not proof, though, that it couldn't be done. The pure rationalist would say that you're using that as a justification for your religion, which may be fine, as long as you don't pretend that it's in fact the state of affairs. So much of the project of science is to subtract the relative and the subjective from the real state of affairs. So the project of a scientist, as he or she might describe it, is not to create a meaningful life, but to get an accurate picture of life and of the world surrounding life.

FOERST: Well if any rationalist would actually say this to me, I would say to him or her, "Baby, you have ignored what's happened in the last thirty years in science and epistemology." Because it started with Thomas Kuhn, then it went over to Bruno Latour. Then in the seventies we had the whole development of radical constructivism within computer and cognitive sciences. Scientists have recognized that objectivity is a dream. Have you read Thomas S. Kuhn's book *The Structure of Scientific Revolutions*? He describes all these things when he defines the paradigm as constructed scientific theory, which includes, besides models and symbols, values and non-empirical assumptions. There are these scientists who think they are so objective and they know it all: they know that there is phlogiston around. They all believe in it; it is true for them. And then suddenly someone comes and says, "Hey! There is something like oxygen in the air!"

There is no such thing as pure objectivity. I don't want to hide from the attempt to come up with a unifying theory, but I know, and the whole epistemology has been done. Really, this is one of the few things that seem to be pretty much proved:

that there will be a lot of unifying theories, and every one will be totally coherent in itself. And every one will be based on a certain set of assumptions. My whole training is to find out those assumptions. And I can always lay those down and say, "If I don't buy this one, I'll come up with another unifying theory." So, if a pure rationalist would say this to me, I could show him that he or she – no it would be a man actually – I could show him that he is wrong.

SLACK: I certainly know a lot of scientists who do hold that view. It's not quite that basic, but they would say that the object referred to in the word "objectivity" may never be completely described, but that it is there. This is clearly a Kantian view, that there is a noumenal reality and that the reality we humans live in is best when it is both as complete as possible and as coherent as possible. That's what we can work toward and that's what we call truth at any given time. So you take your most complete and most coherent theory and see how well it works. And the better it works, the closer you are to what they call the truth.

FOERST: If you express it this way, I would agree. I think the whole scientific enterprise is based on this, and has to be based on this. That's fine because that's a very relativist concept of truth. If you phrase it this way, it's fine. If you phrase it like you did at the beginning, people then go a step further and say, "Therefore religion is wrong." Then they give up their relativist concept of truth and make their truth and their method into an ultimate and totally and absolutely true thing. Then they ignore everything. Then they become rationalist fanatics and are as "religious" as Creationists.

SLACK: Well, I've got to say this has been really interesting and fun for me. Thank you very much.

FOERST: Your questions were great! Thank you.

Further reading

Many of the following books were mentioned in the preceding pages. The others might also be of interest to readers wanting to follow up the ideas expressed by the scientists in the interviews.

Barbour, I. (1997) *Religion and Science*, New York: HarperCollins.

Barrow, J. (1990) *The World Within the World*, Oxford: Oxford University Press.

Barrow, J. (1996) *The Anthropic Cosmological Principle*, Oxford: Oxford University Press,

Cobb, J. (1998) *Cybergrace*, New York: Crown Books.

Davies, P. (1983) *God and the New Physics*, New York: Simon and Schuster.

Davies, P. (1992) *The Mind of God: The Scientific Basis for a Rational World*, New York: Simon and Schuster.

Dawkins, R. (1996) *The Blind Watchmaker: Why the Evidence of Evolution Reveals a Universe Without Design*, W.W. New York: Norton & Company.

de Duve, C. (1995) *Vital Dust*, New York: HarperCollins.

Dennett, D. C. (1995) *Darwin's Dangerous Idea: Evolution and the Meanings of Life*, New York, Simon and Schuster.

Eliade, M. (1959) *The Sacred and the Profane: The Nature of Religion*, New York: Harcourt, Brace.

Ellis, G. F. R. and Murphy N. (1996) *The Moral Nature of the Universe*, Minneapolis: Fortress Press.

Golshani, M. (1997) *From Physics to Metaphysics*, Tehran: Institute for Humanities and Cultural Studies.

Golshani, M. (1997) *The Holy Qur'an and the Sciences of Nature. Studies in Contemporary Philosophical Theology*, Binghamton/Salt Lake City: Binghamton University/Brigham Young University.

Golshani, M. (ed.) (1998) *Can Science Dispense with Religion?* Tehran: Institute for Humanities and Cultural Studies.

Goodenough, U. (1998) *The Sacred Depths of Nature*, New York: Oxford University Press.

Jürgen, M. (1993) *God in Creation: A New Theology of Creation and the Spirit of God*, Minneapolis: Fortress Press.

Matt, D. C. (1996) *God and the Big Bang: Discovering Harmony Between Science and Spirituality*, Woodstock, VT: Jewish Lights Publishing.

Matthews, C. N. and Varghese, R. A. (eds.) (1994) *Cosmic Beginnings and Human Ends: Where Science and Religion Meet*, Chicago: Open Court.

National Academy of Sciences (US) (1984) *Science and Creationism: A View from the National Academy of Sciences*, Washington DC: National Academy Press.

Overbye, D. (1991) *Lonely Hearts of the Cosmos*, New York: Harper-Collins.

Peacocke, A. (1984) *Intimations of Reality*, Notre Dame: University of Notre Dame Press.

Penzias, A. (1989) *Ideas and Information*, New York: Simon and Schuster.

Pesce, M. (2000) *The Playful World: How Technology is Transforming Our Imagination*, New York: Ballantine Books.

Polkinghorne, J. (1998) *Belief in God in an Age of Science*, New Haven: Yale University Press.

Pollack, R. (1999) *The Missing Moment: How the Unconscious Shapes Modern Science*, New York: Houghton Mifflin.

Richardson, W. M. and Wesley J. W. (eds.) (1996) *Religion & Science: History, Method, Dialogue*, New York: Routledge.

Richardson, W. M., Russell, R. J., Clayton, P. and Wegter-McNelly, K. (eds.) (forthcoming) *Science and the Spiritual Quest: New Essays by Leading Scientists*, New York: Routledge.

Sagan, C. (1995) *The Demon-Haunted World: Science as a Candle in the Dark*, New York: Random House.

Scholem, G. G. (1995) *Major Trends in Jewish Mysticism*, New York: Schocken Books.

Schroeder, G. L. (1990) *Genesis and the Big Bang: The Discovery of Harmony Between Modern Science and the Bible*, New York: Bantam Books.

Smith, B. C. (1996) *On the Origin of Objects*, Cambridge, Mass.: MIT Press.

Weinberg, S. (1992) *Dreams of a Final Theory*, New York: Pantheon Books.

Winner, L. (1986) *The Whale and the Reactor: In Search for Limits in an Age of High Technology*, Chicago: University of Chicago Press.